LEADERSHIP SKILLS
FOR
DEPARTMENT CHAIRS

LEADERSHIP SKILLS
FOR
DEPARTMENT CHAIRS

Walter H. Gmelch
Washington State University

Val D. Miskin
Washington State University

Anker Publishing Company, Inc.
Bolton, MA

Leadership Skills For Department Chairs

ISBN 0–9627042–6–1

Composition by Deerfoot Studios.
Cover Design by Marianna Montuori.

Anker Publishing Company, Inc.
176 Ballville Road
P.O. Box 249
Bolton, MA 01740–0249

DEDICATION

To our families…
for their patience, support and understanding.

Paula Gmelch and Wendy Miskin, whose examples provide
the inspiration of leadership.

Blake, Jenny, Deborah, Kim and Greg Miskin, and
Ben and Tom Gmelch, who have taught us that
leadership is a shared experience.

ABOUT THE AUTHORS

Walter H. Gmelch is professor and chair of the Educational Administration Department at Washington State University, where he also serves as Director of the National Center for the Study of the Department Chair. He earned his Ph.D. in the Educational Executive Program from the University of California-Santa Barbara, MBA from the University of California-Berkeley, and Bachelor's from Stanford University. An educator, management consultant, university administrator and former business executive, Dr. Gmelch has conducted research and written extensively on the topics of leadership, team development, conflict, stress and time management. He is one of the leading researchers in the study of department chairs in higher education, serving as editor of two journals and on the editorial board of a half dozen others, as well as directing two national studies of university department chairs and another investigation of community college chairs. He has presented hundreds of workshops on these topics throughout the world and is the author of several books.

Val D. Miskin is Director of Graduate Programs in the College of Business and Economics at Washington State University. He received his Ph.D. in administration from Washington State University, MBA from Utah State University, and Bachelor's in psychology from Brigham Young University. A one-time business owner, Dr. Miskin has over fifteen years of corporate managerial experience in management training and leadership development. He has presented papers at numerous national conferences, published in a variety of management journals, and has written several books. He teaches and consults in the areas of strategic leadership and human resource management.

CONTENTS

INTRODUCTION

Did you accept the position of department chair without leadership training, without a vision for creating tomorrow's program, without a clear understanding of the time demands, conflict and stress inherent to the position, and without an awareness of the demands on your academic career and personal life? Most chairs do!

These considerations challenge the estimated 80,000 academic department chairs across the country responsible for the management of the *production units* of colleges and universities. Since nearly 80 percent of all administrative decisions in higher education are made at the department level, it becomes imperative that our colleges and universities search for department chairs with a sense of commitment, not just a passing interest, and with leadership ability, not just a sense of duty.

Caught between conflicting interests of faculty scholarship and department administration, chairs face the challenge of merging the individual interests with the department goals. While they champion the values of their faculty, at the same time they must mediate the concerns of administration. "Rooted in the faculty like no other administrator but tied to the administration like no other faculty member, the chair has both an excess and deficiency of identity" (Bennett, 1983, p. 3).

This book addresses three major challenges facing department chairs:

(1) To develop an understanding and clarity about the motives and roles of a department chair. Chapter One assists in understanding and assessing your motives and Chapter Two provides guidance in developing your role as department team leader.

(2) To understand the strategic planning process for creating a productive department Chapter Three discusses the value of a

long-term planning focus and Chapter Four takes you through the planning steps for implementing your department plans.

(3) To develop the key leadership skills required to be an effective department chair. Chapters Five, Six, and Seven explore the skills to effectively manage your time, creatively resolve your conflict, and transform your distress to positive and productive stress. Chapter Eight introduces the department chair trade-offs and pay-offs to achieve your optimum balance.

The capacity to meet all three of these challenges exists within you. But you must foster your ability to make the radical shift from a discipline specialist to an academic leader, from an individual scholar to a leader of scholars, and from a loyalist to the discipline to a strategic planner for the department. With interest and enthusiasm to this commitment, you can maintain your academic integrity and yet respond to the call for department leadership.

PREFACE

This book represents our attempt to bring about a greater awareness and visibility of the importance of effective departmental leadership. It does not represent another general management book to be shelved along with the already prolific and popular writings on management. The department chair position is unique among management positions. This book is written specifically for you, the department chair, to help you and your faculty members build bridges between individual achievement and department productivity.

The information shared in this book is derived from three main sources. First, the trials and tribulations from conducting workshops for higher education administrators has given us insight into what realistically does and does not work. Second, the authors' firsthand management experience in corporations and institutions of higher education has provided insight into the realm of academic leadership. As business executives, professors, department chairs, program managers, management consultants and researchers, we share our experiences and knowledge about the common denominators of departmental leadership. Finally, the book integrates the most current research and writings on department chairs, including the authors' recent research investigating the dimensions and dilemmas of department chairs.

Since books written for academics must be grounded in sound research, it seems appropriate to provide further explanation of the research studies conducted and guided by the authors through the Center for the Study of the Department Chair at Washington State University. In the Spring of 1989, the University Council for Educational Administration approved the establishment of the Center for the Study of the Department Chair at Washington State University. With partial funding by UCEA and substantial support from the Danforth Foundation, the Center team of researchers embarked on a series of studies to fulfill the mission of the Center.

Five studies have now been conducted. Two of the studies involved over 1,600 department chairs in over 150 colleges and universities throughout the United States. A response rate of over 70 percent was achieved in both national studies. In addition, a similar study of a single institution was conducted and two ethnographic studies investigated the transition to department chair and the commitment of department chairs to leadership. From our studies we now understand more about how chairs view themselves, their sacrifices, and their challenges.

We would especially like to acknowledge the Center research team of Jack Burns, Jim Carroll, Salli Harris, Rita Seedorf and Diane Wentz for their contributions to the expansion of the theoretical and practical understanding of the position of department chair. The tireless work and selfless dedication to the field of leadership in higher education is an inspiration to doctoral students and professors alike.

We acknowledge with gratitude our dedicated and proficient support staff for their assistance throughout this project: Janet McGough, Tracy Schellenberg, Lynn Buckley and Patti Komp.

Finally, the transformation from first draft to final manuscript was aided by critical reviews and helpful comments from colleagues in the field: William E. Cashin, Kansas State University; Calline Ellis, Westark Community College; Michael J. Galgano, James Madison University; Irene Hecht, American Council on Education; Robert Hogan, University of Tulsa; Martha M. McCarthy, Indiana University; Forrest W. Parkay, Washington State University; and Bruce Partin, Roanoke College.

Further information regarding any of these studies can be obtained by contacting: the Center for the Study of the Department Chair, Cleveland Hall, Washington State University, Pullman, WA 99164-2136.

Part I

Understanding the Challenges of Department Chairs

Have you accepted the call for department leadership? It requires you to transform your interests and role from academic scholar to administrator. Effective department chairs must change and grow with this opportunity, as it requires a long-term focus on staff, faculty and outcomes.

Chapters One and Two introduce you to the challenge of leading an academic department and to the reward of developing a productive, collaborative and supportive department team. Building a collective team climate within the department will enhance both your productivity and enjoyment.

1

THE CALL FOR LEADERSHIP

Even if you're on the right track, you'll get run over if you just sit there.

— Will Rogers

The position of department chair is one of leadership, charged with the challenges of developing the department's future and of building faculty vitality. As we move into the new millennium, we face a time of major change for the over 3,000 universities and colleges in the United States. Changing student clientele, disintegrating college curricula, growing technological changes, and shifting attitudes and practices of faculty represent some of the many forces currently shaping higher education.

Change is inevitable. But the critical question is how well chairs and departments prepare for it and position themselves to survive and succeed. Your success in these changing times requires a clear sense of the future (a focus on what your department can become) and the personal leadership skills to shape the future (what type of leader you can become). Anticipating your changing environments, developing a future-oriented statement of department mission, and providing leadership to unify department activity toward a "planned" future is the mark of effective academic leaders. Dean Rom Markin of the College of Business and Economics at Washington State University gives emphasis to this leadership challenge:

Truly successful people learn that managing change is an exercise in self mastery. They also learn that self mastery comes about by a process of personal and professional growth which embraces ready acceptance of new knowledge and a desire to always be a student, open and seeking information. Such people know that the illiterate are not those who can't read or write, but those who stop learning. Those who manage change well are those who have high expectations and are optimistic about succeeding—attitudes proven to be positive elements of success. Finally, survivors and successful managers of change are always creating alternative futures, contingency plans, rainy day funds, and other strategies that assure survival. In times of descent as well as ascent, it's always well to revisit the personal or professional mission statement. (1992, p. 1)

The time of "amateur administration" where professors temporarily step into the administrative role of department chair has lost its effectiveness. The call for leadership is real. Department chairs are critical to the future of the college, department and faculty.

This chapter addresses the why, what and how of the leadership call. In essence, it attempts to answer three basic questions: Why become a department chair? What do department chairs do? and How can you become an effective chair? Chapter Two then completes this leadership question with a discussion of developing your department into an academic team.

WHY BE A DEPARTMENT CHAIR?

Given the complications and ambiguities of the chair position, why do faculty members choose to serve in this capacity? What are the real motives faculty members have for accepting the position, and does this motivation affect their willingness to be a leader?

As you examine your own motives, it may help to see responses from others concerning their decision to become department chairs. Three studies conducted by the Center for the Study of the Department Chair at Washington State University, using both interviews and surveys, may give insight to this decision and how it affects the leadership role (see Preface). When chairs across the United states were asked what motivated them to become department chairs, they basically responded in two ways.

Extrinsic Motivation

Some chairs chose to serve for *extrinsic* reasons: their dean or colleagues convinced them to take the job or they felt forced to take it because no one else was willing to take on the responsibility or could do the job properly. Typical extrinsically motivated testimonials indicated they were requested to, told to, or approached by the dean. One chair said: "Temporary insanity (only kidding); the dean approached me—said he thought I had a lot of skills that were needed and that I could do a good job" (Seedorf, 1990). Other chairs were persuaded by their peers because "no one else had a suitable combination of seniority, respect and personality." Some chairs took the position because they felt that they could do a better job than other faculty: "No one who would be a good chair was interested," or "None of those who were interested were, in my opinion, capable of being a good chair—I was scared to death of the alternative!"

Intrinsic Motivation

In contrast, many chairs sought the position for *intrinsic* reasons: they saw it as an opportunity to help either the department or themselves. Those who expressed the altruistic need to help the department stated that they "desired to help other faculty members," "wanted to build a strong academic department," or "needed to help develop a new program in the department." Others who were more motivated by personal reasons sought the chair position because they "needed a challenge," "required the financial gain (if there really is any!)," "desired to try something new…in addition to teaching and research," "wanted administrative experience in order to take the next step in the career ladder" or simply "wanted to be in more control of (their) environment."

Does the initial motivation affect the chair's ability or willingness to serve? In the national survey, hundreds of chairs answered the following two questions: What was your motivation to serve? and Are you willing to serve more than one term? The results, reported in Table 1.1, indicate that chairs most frequently served

Table 1.1
Why Faculty Became Department Chairs

Reason for Serving	No. Chairs
1. For personal development (interesting challenge, new opportunities)	321
2. Drafted by the dean or my colleagues	251
3. Out of necessity (lack of alternative candidates)	196
4. To be more in control of my environment	161
5. Out of sense of duty, it was my turn	133
6. For financial gain	117
7. An opportunity to relocate at new institution	101

Source: Center for the Study of the Department Chair, Washington State University, 1992.

for personal development reasons (321 chairs or 60 percent). However, 251 or 46.8 percent of the chairs said they also were drafted by their dean or colleagues. These were the two most frequent reasons for serving as department chair, the first represents an intrinsic motivation to serve and the latter an extrinsic motivation.

In response to the second question, 46 percent of the chairs indicated a willingness to serve another term as chair, 30 percent said they would not, and 24 percent were still undecided (Figure 1.1). What is interesting is that those who agreed to serve primarily for extrinsic reasons were the least likely to serve another term (only 25 percent, see Figure 1.2). In contrast, three-quarters (75 percent) of the intrinsically motivated chairs were willing to serve again (Figure 1.3). These results demonstrate that by a three-to-one margin, those most willing to continue in the chair position had taken the position for personal-intrinsic reasons.

Regardless of your initial reasons for agreeing to serve as chair, your current motivation and commitment to continue in administration will influence your ability to develop leadership capacity. Reflect for a moment and indicate in Exercise 1.1 the primary reasons you became a department chair.

Exercise 1.1
Why Be a Department Chair?

Indicate below the reasons why you became department chair. You may check more than one.

___ 1. For personal development (challenge, new opportunities)

___ 2. To be in more control of my environment

___ 3. For financial gain

___ 4. Drafted by the dean or my colleagues

___ 5. Out of a sense of duty, it was my turn

___ 6. Out of necessity (lack of alternative candidate)

Now compare your responses with those of other chairs in Table 1.1.

Figure 1.1
Chairs' Willingness to Serve Another Term

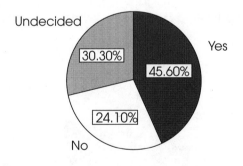

If No (160)	If Yes (241)
Dislike job (20%)	Finish Tasks (72%)
Served Long Enough (58%)	Undecided Career Move (8%)
Other (22%)	Other (20%)

Source: Center for the Study of the Department Chair, Washington State University, 1990.

Figure 1.2
Chairs Motivated by Extrinsic Reasons

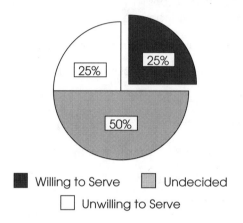

Source: Center for the Study of the Department Chair, Washington State University, 1990.

Figure 1.3
Chairs Motivated by Personal-Intrinsic Reasons

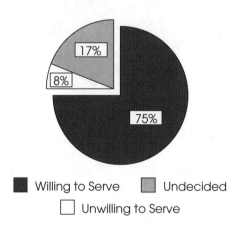

Source: Center for the Study of the Department Chair, Washington State University, 1990.

With the leadership crisis which currently exists in higher education, it is critical for department chairs to answer this leadership call. There needs to be continuity in the chair position, not just taking one's "turn." The position of department chair is too critical to the effectiveness of the institution, the faculty, the community, and to you personally to serve solely from a sense of duty. Your sense of duty must be combined with a real interest and commitment to the position and its challenges and responsibilities.

WHAT DO CHAIRS DO?

No doubt you keep busy as department chair. Endless meetings, stacks of paperwork, constant interruptions, and fragmented encounters on a multitude of topics set a frantic pace. But to what end? All the memos, meetings, phone calls, drop-in visitors and confrontations represent means, but do these activities produce the desired ends?

You must understand that effective chairs influence the future of their departments. It is the focus on results that successfully moves departments through these changing times. Virtually every managerial book written lists and exults the tasks, duties, roles and responsibilities of administrators, from the traditional Peter Drucker approach of planning, organizing, staffing, delegating and controlling, to Warren Bennis's four elements of transformational leadership: attention through vision, meaning through communication, trust through positioning, and the deployment of self (Bennis and Nanus, 1985).

Lists specific to department chair duties range from the exhaustive listing of 97 activities discovered by a University of Nebraska research team (Creswell, et al., 1990), or the astonishing 54 varieties of tasks and duties cited in Allan Tucker's classic book *Chairing the Academic Department* (1992), or the 40 functions forwarded in a study of Australian department chairs (Moses and Roe, 1990). The genesis of these lists can be traced back to Siever's 12 functions, expanded to 18 by McCarthy, reduced to 15 by Hoyt, and expanded again to 27 by Smart and Elton (Moses and Roe, 1990).

Typical faculty manuals at most colleges and universities provide a list of the chairs' duties and responsibilities, such as organizing and supervising curriculum, distributing teaching research loads, supervising department funds, recommending promotions and salaries, and so on. Check your college manual for your own local listings! While these numerous lists appear refined and comprehensive, they continue to represent frag- mented activities without focus on the bottom line—the results.

The Four Roles of Department Chairs

What roles are critical for department chairs to achieve results? In answer to this question, four main department chair roles emerge from the popular literature and converge with current research: the Faculty Developer, Manager, Leader, and Scholar.

The role of *Faculty Developer* is viewed by department chairs as their most important responsibility. This involves the tasks of the recruitment, selection and evaluation of faculty as well as pro- viding the informal faculty leadership to enhance faculty morale and their professional development.

Acting as a *Manager*, the second role, is a requirement of the position, but often least liked by chairs (McLaughlin, et al. 1975). Chairs spend over half their week in department activities. Specif- ically, they perform maintenance functions of preparing budgets, maintaining department records, assigning duties to faculty, supervising non-academic staff, and maintaining finances, facili- ties and equipment.

Leader best describes the third role of department chairs. As leaders of their department they provide long-term direction and vision for the department, solicit ideas to improve the department, plan and evaluate curriculum development, and plan and con- duct departmental meetings. They also provide the external lead- ership for their departments by working with their constituents to coordinate department activities, represent the department at professional meetings, and, on behalf of the department, partici- pate in college and university committees to keep faculty informed of external concerns. Chairs seem to like this role because of opportunities to help others develop professional skills, to have a challenging job, and to influence the profession and department. And those chairs who enjoy these leadership activities spend more time performing them—not a surprising revelation! (McLaughlin, et al. 1975) It is our hope that not only do department chairs enjoy this role but that they take it most seriously when assuming their administrative position. Since it is the most critical role to achieve success, the entire second section of this book is devoted to this call to leadership.

In contrast to the managerial nature of the three previous department chair roles, chairs also try to remain a *Scholar* while serving as chair. This role includes the continuing need to teach and keep current in their academic discipline and, for those in research universities, maintain an active research program and obtain grants to support their research. Chairs enjoy and feel most comfortable in this role (McLaughlin, et al. 1975), but express frustration in their inability to spend much time with their academic interests. Many would spend more time on their own academic activities if they could, but find it virtually impossible. In fact, 86 percent of department chairs significantly reduce their scholarly activities while serving as chair, and for some their scholarship virtually ceases.

Where do your primary interests lie? Exercise 1.2 enables you to assess the degree to which you feel each of these four department chair roles is important to you in your current position. In order to obtain a sense of identity, reflect for a moment on how you ranked the four roles, then look within each role and identify the most important tasks you perform to obtain your results. Is your perception in line with the reality of obtaining results in your job? You may have to realign some of your time and energies to maximize your results. These adjustments should be made consciously as you assume the administrative role of department chair. The transition from the professorial role to that of department chair is vital to your success.

HOW CAN YOU BE AN EFFECTIVE CHAIR?

While it would be convenient to move immediately into your leadership role, the transformation from professor to chair takes time and dedication. Not all chairs make the complete transition to leadership. They try to maintain their faculty responsibilities during their time in office and engage in both types of work simultaneously, resulting in what one researcher discovered as: "the work of administration and the work of the professor do not make good bedfellows....The nature of administrative work is varied, brief and fragmented and, therefore, the administrator cannot devote long periods of uninterrupted time to single issues. The nature of professorial work demands long periods of time to

Exercise 1.2
Department Chair Role

Chair Role

A.   Listed below are 24 typical duties of department chairs. Please answer the
     following questions for each of the duties listed.

	How important to you is each chair duty?				
	Low				High

Leader

Coordinate departmental activities with constituents	1	2	3	4	5
Plan and evaluate curriculum development	1	2	3	4	5
Solicit ideas to improve the department	1	2	3	4	5
Represent the department at professional meetings	1	2	3	4	5
Provide informal faculty leadership	1	2	3	4	5
Develop and initiate long-range vision and departmental goals	1	2	3	4	5

Scholar

Obtain resources for personal research	1	2	3	4	5
Maintain research program and associated professional activities	1	2	3	4	5
Remain current within academic discipline	1	2	3	4	5
Obtain and manage external funds (grants, contracts)	1	2	3	4	5
Select and supervise graduate students	1	2	3	4	5
Teach and advise students	1	2	3	4	5

Faculty Developer

Encourage professional development efforts of faculty	1	2	3	4	5
Encourage faculty research and publication	1	2	3	4	5
Recruit and select faculty	1	2	3	4	5
Maintain conductive work climate, including reducing conflicts	1	2	3	4	5
Evaluate faculty performance	1	2	3	4	5
Represent department to administration	1	2	3	4	5

Manager

Prepare and propose budgets	1	2	3	4	5
Plan and conduct department meetings	1	2	3	4	5

Manage department resources (finances, facilities,
    equipment)   1   2   3   4   5

Assure the maintenance of accurate department
    records   1   2   3   4   5

Manage non-academic staff   1   2   3   4   5

Assign teaching, research and other related duties
    to faculty   1   2   3   4   5

Department Chair Role Orientation Scoring

The Department Chair Orientation instrument is keyed to four different roles department chairs perform.

B.   Add your total score for each role. Plot your scores on the appropriate axes below, then connect the points with straight lines to get a visual representation of your dominant and back-up chair orientations.

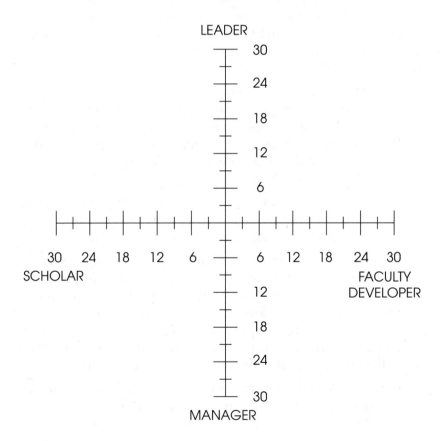

concentrate on issues, to write and see a work through to publication, and to prepare to teach, and evaluate classes" (Seedorf, 1990, pp. 122-123). Therefore, you must let go of your previous professorial role, at least in part, in order to successfully make this transition. This underscores the importance of wanting to serve for the right reasons. Intrinsic motivation may indeed be a prerequisite to accepting the leadership challenge.

Transitions to Leadership

The drastic differences between the two roles of scholar and administrator help explain the difficulty in making the transition to department chair. As this transformation, aptly termed the "metamorphosis of the department chair" takes place, several of your "faculty" functions and work habits change into "chair" work styles (Gmelch and Seedorf, 1989). These new chair work styles are much different from what you were used to as a faculty member and will take some adjustment. The following list outlines nine transitions you face when moving from a faculty position to department chair.

1. *From solitary to social.* College professors typically work alone on research, teaching preparation, and projects. Now, as chair, your responsibility forces you to work with and through others. For example, department goals cannot be achieved alone, they must be achieved in concert with your faculty.

2. *From focused to fragmented.* While professors must have long, uninterrupted periods to work on scholarly pursuits, your work as department chair, like other management positions, is characterized by brevity, variety and fragmentation.

3. *From autonomy to accountability.* Professors generally enjoy control over their time and the feeling of autonomy of activity and movement in their working environment. As you move from your role of professor to administrator you tend to lose this sense of autonomy and become accountable to upper administration and the faculty for your time and accessibility in the office, as well as for your actions and activities.

4. *From manuscripts to memoranda.* The scholar and researcher labors over a manuscript for a long period of time. Before finding printers ink, the work goes through many revisions

and critiques. As department chair you quickly must learn the art of persuasion and precision through memos. Thus, chairs report less stress from manuscripts and more from completing paperwork on time (Chapter Seven).

5. *From private to public.* The professor may block out long periods of time for scholarly work while as chair you have an obligation to be accessible throughout the day to the many publics you serve. In essence, you move from the privilege of a "closed door" to the obligation of an "open door" policy.

6. *From professing to persuading.* In the academic profession, the professor is disseminating information in a manner that will meet the learning objectives of others. As you turn from professor into chair you profess less and practice more the art of persuasion and compromise.

7. *From stability to mobility.* While always growing and exploring new concepts and ideas, faculty generally experience movement within the stability of their discipline and circle of professional associations. As a chair you also attempt to retain your professional identity but must become mobile within the university structure. In order to be at the cutting edge of educational reform and implement needed programmatic changes within, you must be more mobile, visible, and political.

8. *From client to custodian.* In relation to university resources, the professor is a client, requesting and expecting resources to be available to conduct research, classes, and service activities. As chair you represent the custodian and dispenser of resources and are responsible for the maintenance of the physical setting as well as providing material and monetary resources.

9. *From austerity to prosperity.* While in actuality the pay differential between professor and chair may not be significant, the perception of more control over departmental resources creates the illusion of greater prosperity as chair.

Rather than listing these transitions in a table, visualize in Figure 1.4 the professor at the inner core of a set of concentric circles. The professor is characterized in this inner circle as focused, autonomous, private, stable, solitary, austere, and a client of the department. The metamorphosis transforms these professorial inner traits into an other-oriented (outer circle), creating an administrative profile of social, fragmented, accountable, public, mobile, prosperous, and custodial. These outwardly expanding circles represent the types of transitions needed to successfully move from a faculty member to administrative responsibility and challenge. You must recognize the fundamental differences between the roles of academic professor and department chair.

Figure 1.4
The Transformation from Professor to Chair

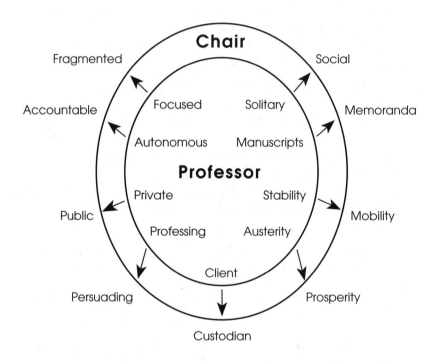

ARE YOU READY FOR DEPARTMENT LEADERSHIP?
Leading with Diversity

We are now a part of a new management era with more women in upper levels of corporations and higher education (Naisbitt and Aburdene, 1990). For example, in doctorate-granting institutions today about 10 percent of the department chairs are female. Twenty years ago when most of these women were receiving their doctorates, only 13 percent of the doctorates were being granted to women. In contrast, currently 37 percent of doctorates are granted to women (Bowen and Schuster, 1986), which implies that the percentage of female department chairs will increase as this group of graduates accept leadership positions in institutions of higher education.

Understanding the value of gender and diversity in higher education is of growing importance. To explain the intricacies and complexity of diversity in organizations requires a theory and vocabulary. For example, Rosabeth Moss Kanter's book, *Men and Women of the Corporation* (1977), sheds light on the significance numbers play in leadership. As it applies to institutions of higher education, group dynamics is impacted by the proportional representation of different kinds of faculty or chairs in a meeting, whether it be by gender, race, ethnicity or any other significant influence. For example, "uniform" groups have only one kind of person and are considered homogeneous with respect to salient status such as race, gender, or ethnicity. This homogeneously significant type, called "dominants," controls the group or department and its culture. At the other extreme, "skewed" departments occur when there is a preponderance of one type over another. The few in a skewed group, called "tokens," are often treated as representatives of their category; as symbols rather than individuals. Even if a college or division has more than one token in a skewed department (e.g., two women or minorities), it is difficult for them to generate an alliance or to gain power positions in the department.

However, the importance in having diverse participation in groups is not so much in the numbers or proportions they represent, but the *perspective* they bring to the events (Dillard, 1992). Diverse representation in department chair positions not only provides important role models but introduces broader variety in management styles to accommodate more diverse perspectives. A true team climate is based on multiple perspectives.

Leadership Self-Assessment

Regardless of gender, minority status or ethnic heritage, improving your leadership capacity will:

- Value diversity in experience and talent;
- Encourage staff to participate and satisfy their interests; and
- Build a collective team climate.

An honest self-appraisal of your management style can be most beneficial in assessing how ready you are for this leadership challenge. Rate yourself on the items in Exercise 1.3. Express your current attitudes toward openness, recognition, diverse perspectives, and faculty development and you will discover your readiness to enjoy your role as department chair. These ratings give an overall indication of your willingness to accept leadership responsibilities while maintaining the respect of your faculty members.

Calculate your score by adding the total items checked in each of the four columns. Then multiply the first column total by 1, the total of column two by 2, column three by 3, and the last column to the right by 4. Adding these new totals together will give you your "department leadership" score.

If you score below 25, you may want to set some specific improvement goals for yourself. A score of 35 or above indicates a strong foundation for guiding your faculty's and department's vitality. You are now on your way to answering the call to leadership.

Exercise 1.3
Department Leadership Self-Assessment

Required Leadership Behaviors	(1) Not Really	(2) Could Use Improve- ment	(3) Partially True	(4) Very True
A. Able to show visible enthusiasm for almost all duties of the department chair.	____	____	____	____
B. Willing to put in significant extra time if necessary to pre- pare for an upcoming faculty meeting.	____	____	____	____
C. Able to put in considerably more work than any other fac- ulty members without feeling resentment.	____	____	____	____
D. Able to direct attention and efforts toward department goals even at the expense of own personal interests.	____	____	____	____
E. Recognize the benefit of diverse perspectives and participation even if it means increased conflict.	____	____	____	____
F. Able to give direction when needed without taking over (dominating) the functions of the staff.	____	____	____	____
G. Willing to give attention and praise to all faculty members whenever they are deserving.	____	____	____	____
H. Concerned with each faculty member's current abilities, goals, and attitudes toward department success.	____	____	____	____
I. Willing to rely on the achieve- ments of faculty for own recog- nition from higher management.	____	____	____	____
J. Able to guide all faculty members effectively in new areas.	____	____	____	____
Subtotal	____	____	____	____ =
	(x1)	(x2)	(x3)	(x4)

Total department leadership score _____

2

DEVELOPING AN ACADEMIC TEAM

We may affirm absolutely that nothing great in the world has ever been accomplished without passion.
— *Georg Hegel*

As department chair, you have the authority to give direction and make decisions for your faculty and staff. Or do you? You have the right to evaluate personnel and establish programs. Or do you? You have a standing invitation to interact with the dean and other university administrators. Or do you? This position of department chair is a distinction to your academic career. Or is it? Your answer to these questions will depend on how well you understand your role as chair and to what extent you exercise this responsibility.

Deciding who teaches which courses, which programs will be managed by which staff members, who completes which reports, or even how many sections of each class will be offered are not the leadership decisions that elicit these opportunities. While management decisions are important to department operations, the leadership decisions are *sine qua non* to inspire and unite faculty effort and direction.

Leadership is more than department action planning and operational decision-making. Leadership prescribes a longer-term department future to unify staff activity and faculty effort. Department leadership requires an emotional commitment, it demands competence and confidence. There is truth to the saying:

"It's difficult to lead a cavalry charge if you think you look funny sitting on a horse." Examine your motives for serving, as discussed in Chapter One, and decide how you can "make a difference" to your department. Take time and devote effort now to begin filling your leadership reservoir. Prepare yourself to provide departmental direction, enthusiasm and commitment.

Many recent articles and books on leadership have identified the value of teams and teamwork (Bradford & Cohen, 1984; DeMeuse & Liebowitz, 1981; Gmelch & Miskin, 1984; Kanter, 1983; Lawler, 1986; Parker, 1991; Sullivan, 1988). One specific study reported that schools using the team management style outperformed schools organized hierarchically (Chubb, 1988). These and other studies continue to acclaim the virtues of teams and teamwork, but fail to capture the fervor of the concept.

Teams not only add value, they add enjoyment. A team climate in your department will make the day-to-day problems more tolerable. Your faculty won't always agree with one another; they will have differing interests and may even dislike one another at times. But one unique characteristic of team process is a mutual respect for each other. Productivity improves with team management, but more importantly, a collective team attitude is exciting, rewarding, collaborative and enjoyable. However, you may recognize that some realities of academic organizations contradict the team concept:

- Academic departments are typically discipline driven with multiple faculty interests.

- Faculty traditionally give lip service to department concerns but receive recognition toward tenure and promotion for their individual research or teaching effort.

- Turbulent and changing environments make short-term goals more realistic than long-term ones.

- Institutional goals are multiple, contradictory, unclear and often imposed.

- Stakeholders and constituents are pluralistic, unpredictable and constantly changing.

These factors won't disappear as you introduce a team process, but they will be placed in their proper perspective. While organizational realities may not be easily changed, they can, and should, be anticipated. A collective team attitude enhances relationships, both internal and external, and prevents individual faculty from becoming dysfunctional within the department. Academic departments shouldn't build team effort at the expense of, but rather through, individual scholarship and teaching effectiveness.

Developing team attitude remains your responsibility and requires your passion, commitment, and continuing communication to faculty and staff alike. The critical elements for building your department team climate are:

1. Understanding the characteristics of an effective team (how you know when you have one).

2. Developing the leadership required to encourage team effort (how you influence your faculty in that direction).

TEAM CHARACTERISTICS:
RECOGNIZING TEAM CLIMATE

Perhaps the best way to recognize team attitude is to understand what a team is *not*. Teams do not require all faculty members to meet together every time a department decision needs to be made. Individual faculty seldom have identical interests and aspirations and they don't even agree with one another much of the time. Academic departments do not require homogeneous team players. In fact, it is the diversity of concerns, ideas and interests that contribute most to department success. Recognizing and encouraging the characteristics of "collective team climate" within your department can encourage individual achievement, improve department scholarship and strengthen your faculty relationships.

The team-building literature is filled with descriptions and explanations of the required, necessary or key "characteristics of effectively functioning teams." Dyer (1977) discusses five team development phases, Gmelch and Miskin (1984) present four principles for productive teams, Larson and LaFasto (1989) identify eight properties of effectively functioning teams, and Parker (1991) lists twelve team characteristics. These and other team effectiveness studies may at first seem to confuse rather than explain or focus on how to build your department team. However, a critical review of the team literature reveals a common set of "team" attitudes or characteristics. Nearly all team studies agree that the collective team climate requires:

1. Clearly stated and agreed upon long-term team goals.
2. Actively involved team members and shared management authority.
3. Openly shared information with participative decision-making.
4. Constructive approach to resolving conflict with attention to individual interests.
5. Top priority attention to individual growth and self-development.

Become familiar with these keys to effective teams by examining the comparisons in Table 2.1 of the factors for effective department teams versus those in less effective department organizations.

Table 2.1
Effective Team Characteristics

	Collective Team Attitude	Traditional Department Climate
Goals	• Long-term, future-oriented department goals • Established and modified to give the best possible match between individual goals and department goals • Commitment sought from all members of the department	• Short-term, changing, operational goals • Little consideration given to individual or personal goals • Imposed upon the group by the chair
Management	• A shared responsibility • All faculty members feel responsible for contributing to the department goals • Different members, because of their knowledge or abilities, act as "resource expert" at different times, thus the management roles change as the tasks of the department change	• Delegated by position • Position determines influence • Obedience to authority the accepted norm • Power concentrated in authority positions
Decision-Making	• Information openly shared with all staff and faculty • Decisions reached by consensus	• Information restricted or unavailable • Decisions made by authority • Those in opposition expected

	• All members usually in agreement with final results or outcomes, after all interested parties have been heard and understood • Disagreements usually constructive to reach common understanding and improve conceptual acceptance	to "go along" even though in actual practice they often remain resentful
Conflict	• Conflict and controversy viewed as positive and essential to the problem-solving process • Disagreements may be frequent and candid, but are relatively comfortable • Little evidence of personal attack; criticism is constructive and even supportive in nature • Interests of all parties explored with collaborative search for common solution	• Conflict viewed as a destructive barrier to problem solving and is consciously ignored or suppressed • Disagreements may be suppressed by the chair or "resolved" by a majority vote, which leaves a still unconvinced minority • Criticism embarrassing and tension producing often leading to accommodation or compromise • Emphasis on department position with little attention to the interests of conflicting parties
Professional Development	• Time and effort directed toward developing strong interpersonal relationships and building individual problem-solving skills • Self-actualization encouraged for each individual team member through achievement of department performance goals • Recognition based on individual contribution to department successes through informal feedback	• Emphasis on conformance to "organizational standards" and on group productivity • Rewards and discipline tied to department productivity goals, with little attention to interpersonal relationships or individual skill development

These concepts are most useful when related specifically to your department. The configuration of your faculty, the relationships with and among them, and their individual interests are unique to your department and merit your attention. It's important to feel the "aura" or "spirit" of your whole department. While each factor will vary among individual faculty members, it's helpful to assess the overall collective team climate for each key characteristic.

Complete Exercise 2.1 by first contrasting each "collective team characteristic" with the "traditional department climate." Review the concepts in Table 2.1 and assess your overall department practices for each major characteristic. Place an "X" on the continuum that best represents your current department status.

Exercise 2.1
Assessing Your Department Team Climate

Review the comparison chart in Table 2.1 and for each characteristic, evaluate the status of your department by placing an " X " on the appropriate continuum below.

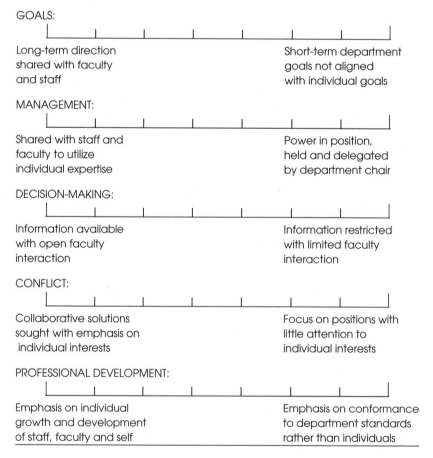

GOALS:

Long-term direction
shared with faculty
and staff

Short-term department
goals not aligned
with individual goals

MANAGEMENT:

Shared with staff and
faculty to utilize
individual expertise

Power in position,
held and delegated
by department chair

DECISION-MAKING:

Information available
with open faculty
interaction

Information restricted
with limited faculty
interaction

CONFLICT:

Collaborative solutions
sought with emphasis on
individual interests

Focus on positions with
little attention to
individual interests

PROFESSIONAL DEVELOPMENT:

Emphasis on individual
growth and development
of staff, faculty and self

Emphasis on conformance
to department standards
rather than individuals

You should appreciate the value of team relationships as an important (and necessary) first step to department leadership. Influencing faculty and department achievement requires your conscious and active involvement. Team leadership implies a new focus to the traditional concept of department management.

TEAM LEADERSHIP: INFLUENCING YOUR FACULTY

The day-to-day activities and programs do not reflect the real challenge of department leadership. In fact, allowing faculty and support staff more autonomy in those areas gives your job more focus. Team leaders don't "do" everything for the department, they provide direction, strengthen relationships and encourage mutual respect (Dyer, 1977; Larson & LaFasto, 1989; Lawler, 1986; Brown, 1988; Andrews, 1986; Miskin & Gmelch, 1985; Parker,1991).

Effective team leaders have a clear role. They continually light the way, and in the process let all individuals see that they do make a difference. Team leaders don't ignore or attempt to reduce individual differences—they unify the future by celebrating individual contributions to the department. Figure 2.1 depicts team leadership as the encompassing support system of the collective department environment. Team leadership not only recognizes, but encourages team process in each major dimension.

**Figure 2.1
Keys to Department Team Climate**

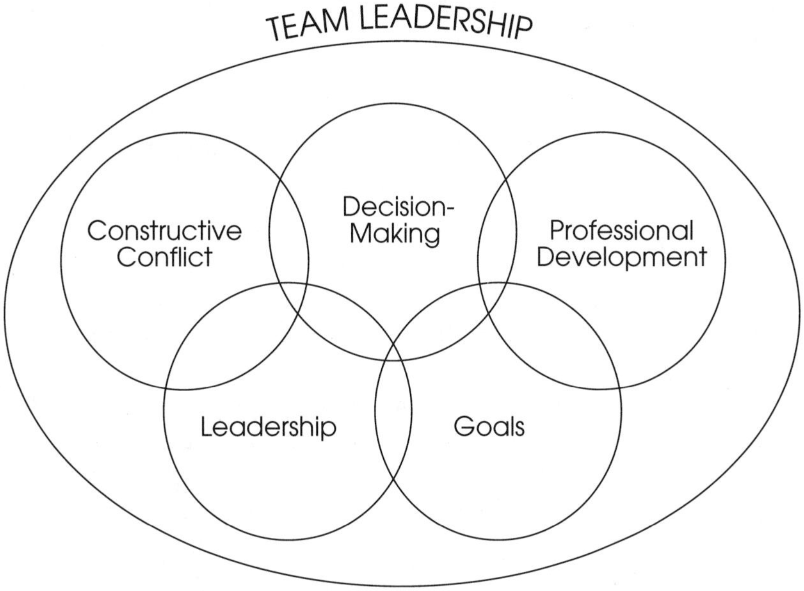

Refer to your evaluation of department team climate in Exercise 2.1. Review your assessment for each characteristic and, for those areas you'd like to see changed, consider your possible leadership options.

Management

The key to collective team process is a sharing of management activities. Faculty members have individual interests and must be encouraged to excel in their scholarly endeavors and at their own initiative. Your role is discussing, sharing, and guiding these in a manner to best contribute to long-term department direction.

Your support staff, on the other hand, have a more direct responsibility to the department and must be challenged to set their individual goals in line with the broad, but shorter-term, department goals. (These management skills are discussed in depth in Chapter Three.)

Goals

Focus on the long-term, guiding future expectations and potential of your department. Encourage individual achievement and direction, but insist the initiative remain with each faculty member. Informally and consistently, as well as at annual review time, share the overarching department goals with your staff and faculty.

The purpose here is to inspire your faculty to set their own challenges and encourage staff to prepare contributing goals—all within the parameters of the longer-term, future-oriented team direction. (This is the topic of Chapter Four.)

Decision-Making

First, establish an open climate of shared information. While it is not practical to send all information to all personnel at all times, develop a climate where all faculty members are willing to ask for (and expect to receive) information as they deem necessary.

Second, build understanding and create acceptance for department decisions. As stated earlier, this does not require a department meeting to be held every time a decision is made. It does, however, require a trust to develop among your faculty that they will be consulted and allowed to impact decisions when pertinent to their interests. (This concept is explored further in Chapter Five.)

Conflict

Conflict, controversy and disagreement are inevitable, but must not become dysfunctional to department success. Explore your faculty's interests and strive to satisfy their needs through collaborative solutions. Encourage this climate informally, constantly and among all individuals in your department. (Chapter Six details the skills for constructive conflict interactions.)

Professional Development

Team effort absolutely depends upon capable, willing and competent faculty members. As team leader, your first priority must be the growth and development of yourself and of each individual staff and faculty member. (Chapters Seven and Eight detail this call for balance and development.) Two simple rules apply:

1. Unleashing individual potential requires conscious challenge and specific encouragement.

2. Meaningful growth is best achieved through active involvement in accomplishing goals.

YOUR LEADERSHIP CHALLENGE

Team leadership adds the "passion" to collective team climate. Your preparation for providing team direction and support to your department is individual and unique; individual to you and your capabilities and unique to your faculty and department situation.

Building a positive and productive department requires conscientious application of time, effort and desire. Approach this challenge with enthusiasm. Become more involved, expand your interests, seek and accept new ideas, and enjoy your new position as you inspire your faculty and staff to greater achievement.

Part II

CREATING A PRODUCTIVE DEPARTMENT

Department leadership focuses on the total organization. It looks beyond daily activities, programs and problems to focus on the overall growth and development of the institution. The critical role of department chairs is to develop and share long-term, future-oriented directions with their staff. This is explained by the four-part "department leadership model" in Figure II which addresses four basic questions common to all academic department chairs:

- Where is your department now?
  (Department Analysis)

- Where do you want your department to be?
  (Department Planning)

- How do you plan to get there?
  (Implementation)

- How well are you doing?
  (Evaluation and Control)

I. Department Analysis

Department leadership begins with and is supported by systematic and continuous scanning of the department's external and internal environments. This information gathering and analysis of salient external environments allows department chairs to anticipate "threats to avoid" and to recognize "opportunities to pursue."

Figure II
Creating a Productive Department

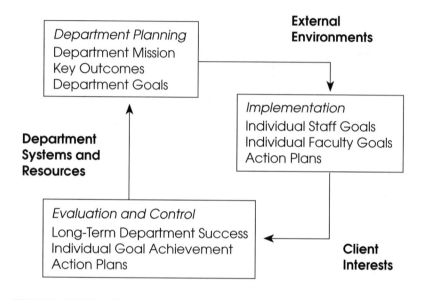

Department Analysis

The chair leadership challenge keys on evaluating your department's internal strengths to provide meaningful direction toward future potential within the department's unique external environments. As shown in Figure II, this analysis is part of the department leadership process and is discussed in further detail in Chapter Three.

II. Department Planning

From information gathered in this analysis, department chairs must translate their conclusions into statements of intent, purpose, and direction to guide the department. Formulating the department's mission statement expresses this overall purpose and gives specificity and direction to this intent. As the planning model indicates, department mission and key outcomes lead to developing collective department goals which is the final topic of Chapter Three.

III. Implementation

The overall, long-term direction of mission statement and key outcomes is a "necessary but not sufficient" condition. Development of individual staff and faculty objectives toward department goals and mission must translate these collective plans into actions. It is this transition from the collective to the individual that activates the team climate described in Chapter Two.

As shown in the department planning model, action planning is the specific vehicle for creating activity toward department goals and encouraging team attitude. It encourages individual development through department achievement and provides the framework for Chapter Four.

IV. Evaluation and Control

Evaluation and feedback is essential to the leadership process. Department chairs must know if and how well the department is moving toward its mission. As the model shows, department control recognizes three priorities.

- First, assessing progress toward overall department success (mission statement and department goals).
- Second, evaluating individual achievement toward department mission (individual staff and faculty goals).
- Third, supporting and encouraging specific activity to accomplish individual goals (action plans).

This process of evaluation and feedback integrates department planning and implementation. It unifies and energizes department activity toward a planned future. And it strengthens relationships as it completes the leadership cycle. This process is discussed in the concluding section of Chapter Four.

3

Department Planning: Analysis and Direction

Which way did they go?
How many were there?
I must find them.
I am their leader.
— Anonymous

W ho is making the leadership decisions for your department? When the dean announces a drive for increased enrollments but denies your request for an additional faculty line—what freedom remains for you to assign faculty workloads? When student enrollments increase dramatically in one area but dwindle in another—where is your flexibility to guide curriculum emphasis? When your advisory board withdraws support for regional fund raising and suggests increasing extramural grant funding—how much can you impact the ultimate direction of your development campaign? When faculty in one discipline initiate new programs and courses—how do you retroactively influence department direction? For answers to these and other "leadership" questions, frequently ask yourself the four basic questions from the Department Leadership Model:

- Where is your department now?
  (Department Analysis)

- Where do you want your department to be?
  (Department Planning)

- How do you plan to get there?
  (Implementation)
- How well are you doing?
  (Evaluation and Control)

Whether new to the chair position or a seasoned veteran faced with new and changing conditions, you need to understand your surroundings. Your department doesn't exist in an isolated lab setting. It is a functioning unit in the institution and continuously impacted by interactions with students, parents, future employers and other constituencies. Data from your changing surroundings are the lifeblood of your department's future. Gathering information from relevant environments requires an ongoing, continuous effort.

DEPARTMENT ANALYSIS:
WHERE IS YOUR DEPARTMENT NOW?

Your charge begins by focusing on the first question: "Where is your department now?" Changes in your broader external environments and your department's varying client interests should be your focus of attention and information gathering.

Your Broader External Environments

Educational institutions do not operate as traditional hierarchies. They are, however, influenced by many of the same forces in the community, nation and world. Monumental changes in both national and world politics are occurring regularly. Astounding technological advances are today's "norms" rather than "exceptions." Major economic fluctuations are becoming the order of the day. These changing forces represent both threats to and opportunities for your department's future.

To gain insight from your department's external environments, systematically consider the following questions:

- What are the current economic projections and how might they impact your enrollments, budgets and faculty recruiting?
- Do you anticipate significant changes in current student enrollments, faculty availability and stakeholder interests?
- What broad social trends do you recognize and what is their significance to your department?

- What new technological developments are occurring that can influence your department?

- Is there any new legislation that has potential to affect your department?

- What values held by other department stakeholders are relevant to your planning process?

- Which areas of teaching specialty are gaining prominence locally, regionally, or nationally?

- What are the trends or new developments in your discipline and academic fields?

- What are other institutions similar to yours doing that has relevance to your planning?

Your Department's Client Interests

The importance of serving the customer (your department's clients) is universally accepted, but the same consensus does not exist for identifying who these customers are. Currently enrolled students are certainly your clients, but their future employers also warrant consideration. In addition, the larger community interests, users of discipline expertise, potential new students and department alums all deserve your attention. Not only can students, potential employers and other department clients identify directions and trends, but they often suggest innovative ideas for new programs, systems, or delivery methods. Identify who your department serves and seek data to clarify clientele interests by systematically addressing the following questions:

- Can your students be described in identifiable groupings?

- What are their specific interests and concerns?

- What do you know about the placement of your graduates?

- What value are you offering to potential students and how is this perceived by them and their employers?

- Which important constituent groups are relevant to your community, discipline and alumni relationships?

- What values held by other department stakeholders are relevant to your planning process?

The signal of declining enrollments is not the time to start learning about your student population. The search for qualified teaching faculty should not be postponed until new faculty lines become available. Fund-raising projects should not be the only impetus for building alumni relationships. Encouraging specific research activity should follow, rather than lead, long-term department direction. Now is your best time to anticipate relevant change and look to the changing conditions of the future.

Your SWOT Analysis

The process of department analysis surveys your department's environments to anticipate its internal *strengths* and *weaknesses* and to identify its external *opportunities* and *threats*. This acronym (SWOT) represents the essence of your department analysis.

While you can't control your external conditions, you must direct your department's internal processes to respond more directly to its changing environments. The value of this analytic preparation is realized as you improve department weaknesses and build on department strengths.

This introspective evaluation allows you to prevent or reduce anticipated threats from external environments. The preeminent value of your analyses lies in capitalizing on department strengths to take advantage of recognized opportunities (Hax & Majluf, 1991; Hamel & Prahalad, 1991; Henry, 1980; Keller, 1983; Porter, 1991; Stoner & Fry, 1987; Thompson & Strickland, 1992). The time required for frequent, formal analyses of your department environments may be prohibitive on a regular basis. However, understanding the systematic process for gathering information from your external and internal environments will prove highly useful. Always be alert for possible threats and potential opportunities from the external environments, and then move to the internal determination of department strengths to meet these challenges.

1. *External Opportunities and Threats.* Threats are defined as any factor outside of your control that may create hardship or difficulty for the department. Changes in the broader economic conditions and in student, employer or community (clients) interests both pose potential threats to your department's success.

Identifying threats can help you avoid investing in declining futures, but recognizing opportunities is the real key to department success. Opportunities can be found in almost every environmental change. In fact, opportunities are frequently just the flip side of threats or problems. For example, when one department faced changes in its national accreditation requirements, they were initially viewed as significant threats to already deficient resources. However, recognizing this change as an opportunity allowed this department to realign and combine two existing programs (not possible under earlier accreditation standards). The external impetus for this change may have gone unnoticed if the department chair had not been prepared for the "opportunity."

2. *Internal Strengths and Weaknesses.* The forces surrounding your department will impact its future. However, it is your department's internal processes that are under your leadership control. Department weaknesses or areas for improvement are described as any department functions or activities that may limit or inhibit its long-term success. As you prepare to consider areas within your department in need of improvement, consider the following questions:

   • Do you see specific patterns of declining enrollments?

   • Are there particular faculty that consistently receive poor teaching evaluations?

   • Do some current research streams fail to support the department's overall interests?

   • Can you identify any individual faculty who are dysfunctional to the overall department?

   • Is your time consumed by nonproductive advisory boards?

It is your answer to these and similar questions that lead to initiating improvement efforts, realigning resources, or even discontinuing selected areas. In contrast, strengths are defined as positive abilities and situations within your department, college, or university that enable your department to take advantage of changes in its external environments. What is your department doing particularly well? How strong is your department "team" climate as discussed in Chapter Two? The following specific questions can assist you in this systematic department review:

- How open, collaborative and supportive are your departmental relationships?

- What are the specific strengths of your individual faculty?

- Which teaching areas are achieving notable enrollments, learning or placement?

- Which current research streams have or promise to have national prominence?

- Which constituents currently provide strong department support?

- What is the outlook for adequate and additional resources?

In short, anything productive your department has that can be continued, strengthened, or built upon should be identified as an internal strength.

Matching Strengths to Opportunities

Specific assessment of areas for improvement is important to resource allocation decisions and specific improvement efforts, but look to your department's strengths as the vital link to your future. As department chair, you need to utilize your most effective faculty's interests and teaching abilities to guide program development. Tie your department's prominent faculty research interests to your long-term goals. Build on existing student quality to develop department relationships with future employers. Utilize your best professional contacts to direct the department's commitment to community partnerships. In Exercise 3.1, specifically analyze your department's internal processes and plan how your department's strengths might be used to take advantage of recognized opportunities identified from your ongoing environment analysis.

The value of this analysis is your increasing awareness of and commitment to the future. Gather your data informally but with conscious intent. The department analysis is your ongoing preparation to give focus to your department planning.

Exercise 3.1
Department Analysis

This analysis should be at your initiative. It can be informal and voluntary, but must include input, critique, and feedback from all relevant stakeholders (faculty, staff, students, dean, constituent groups, etc.).

Identify potential opportunities below and indicate possible options for specifically directing your department's strengths toward them.

Anticipated Opportunities	Potential Options
From changes in your broader external environments:	
From recognition of student, employer, community and other stakeholders interests:	

DEPARTMENT PLANNING:
WHERE DO YOU WANT YOUR DEPARTMENT TO BE?

"Planning for the future is important and I'll get to it just as soon as I get past these current crises." "Inspiring faculty to greater achievement would be a welcome challenge if I didn't have to spend so much time on the little things." "It's so difficult to re-allocate budget when I have to deal with protective faculty attitudes." "Meetings, schedules and deadlines typically preempt my attention to the long-range plan." These expressions from experienced and new department chairs alike, reflect the frustrations often found in managing an academic department. Your challenge is to find a way to attend to these day-to-day department activities and provide the leadership so critical to your department's future. Or, more correctly, your challenge is to provide the leadership so critical to your department's future through these day-to-day management requirements. Your department analysis addressed the question "Where is your department now?" Figure 3.1 introduces the planning element of the department leadership model: "Where do you want your department to be?"

Figure 3.1
Department Leadership Model: Planning

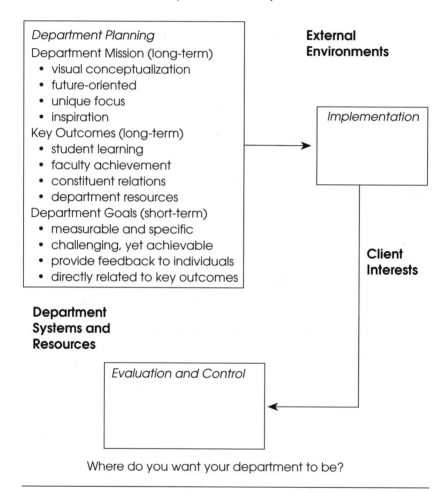

Department Analysis

Department Planning

Department Mission (long-term)
- visual conceptualization
- future-oriented
- unique focus
- inspiration

Key Outcomes (long-term)
- student learning
- faculty achievement
- constituent relations
- department resources

Department Goals (short-term)
- measurable and specific
- challenging, yet achievable
- provide feedback to individuals
- directly related to key outcomes

External Environments

Implementation

Client Interests

Department Systems and Resources

Evaluation and Control

Where do you want your department to be?

Creating Department Vision

During a recent search for a new department chair, one college dean was asked, "What will be your expectations of the new chair?" The dean replied, "The chair will be expected to move this department into its proper future." The dean further explained that the real challenge of chairs is to be aware of their department's past, present, and future surroundings and to give a direction, a focus, and a vision to inspire their faculty and staff toward this future.

This answer clearly identifies the leadership role of the chair position. While the dean's answer included typical statements of scheduling, student learning, faculty involvement, public visibility, etc., the main focus was on the leadership requirement. This concept is given additional clarity with John Diebold's (1984) description of vision.

> Humans need purpose—individually and collectively. Without a sense of purpose, the individual is not only lost but will rapidly disintegrate. Without purpose there is no motivation, no direction, no way to focus the physical and mental faculties of the human. What is true of the individual is even more true of the collective—be it the tribe, the nation, the corporation, the union. What holds the body politic together is the communality of purpose.
>
> When we say "vision," however, we mean more than a commitment to do now what must be done now. Vision implies a purpose beyond the moment, a view of the future, a dreaming and thinking ahead. A vision suggests the imaginative conceptualization of a future that is not inconsistent with the present but that will move the present to something nearer to the ideal (p.401).

What is your role in providing this department vision? One view is that leaders must first create this vision and then persuade others to follow (Bass, 1985; Bennis and Nanus, 1985). An alternative view is that leaders discover a vision that is already present among their constituents and give it articulation (Cleveland, 1985). Other authors suggest that both are likely correct. Vision is more powerfully shared when inspired by the strong personal conviction and motivation of a department leader. Vision becomes richer, however, as it emanates from a variety of faculty, clientele and external sources relevant to the department (Kouzes & Posner, 1987; Nanus, 1992).

Creating or articulating department vision requires frequent and consistent communication. A compelling commitment to a planned future cannot be accomplished casually nor intermittently. Personal and informal explanations can help to create understanding and occasional department meetings will encourage acceptance, but a written mission statement is essential to provide consistent, unifying direction. Much of the literature on organizational "mission statements" defines them as written "statements of purpose" or overall "guiding philosophy statements."

Your mission statement need not be couched in sophisticated rhetoric nor presented in perfect strategic format. To be meaningful, however, it should send a continuous and consistent message concerning the following four elements.

1. *Visual Conceptualization.* Effective department chairs build a picture of what the end result (future potential) will look like. They may not know exactly how they are going to get there, but they have a clear idea of what the department is striving for.

   Your department mission statement must create a visual conceptualization of where the department is heading. Can your faculty "feel" or "see" this department potential and how they will fit into it? As a blueprint to the future, your shared mission statement needs to portray specific images of your department's long-term potential.

2. *Future Orientation.* More than just organizing tasks, setting goals or meeting short-term deadlines, department chairs must have a preoccupation with their future. Staff and faculty typically (and appropriately) operate in the shorter-term. The written mission statement, on the other hand, must conceptualize a future-oriented framework to unite these daily activities and decisions.

   While faculty teaching loads and specific course assignments must be determined each semester, a departmental focus to improve teaching effectiveness requires a two to three year planning transition. Actual time spent on individual faculty research must be continuously encouraged, but a shift in department research paradigms will require three to five years of preparation and planning. Class size and number of sections offered are always immediate concerns, but anticipation of future student and potential employer interests reflect the need for a longer planning focus.

   How well does your mission statement provide this context to unify faculty effort and activity?

3. *Unique Focus.* Department chairs must provide meaningful focus. Does your mission statement communicate a perspective singular to your department's potential? While a written mission statement must, by definition, be visual and future-oriented, it must be particular to your department. Your mission statement should inspire your faculty toward a future unique to your department. It should encourage your staff to capitalize on specific department strengths and take advantage of opportunities in your external environments.

Does your mission statement avoid the use of general platitudes and generic aspirations? How well does it differentiate and distinguish your department's potential and its ability to contribute to the broader goals of your college and university?

4. *Inspiration.* Operational goals accomplish short-term results (what is planned) rather than long-term visions (what we dream about). Department mission statements are visions of the future to inspire creative and exciting short-term achievements. They are alternatives, possibilities, ideals and expressions of optimism and hope. Carefully review your department's mission statement. Is it in writing? Does it exude a sense of the ultimate, a hope for the future, a standard of excellence?

Building a Mission Statement

Can your mission statement really provide this shift from the "organizational" to the "inspirational?" To do so, it must: (a) be in a format that can be shared, (b) contain each of the "vision" elements (visual, future-oriented, unique, inspiring), and (c) be understandable and available to all department personnel.

Consider the following mission statement of a mid-sized department in education: *The mission of the Department of Educational Administration is to establish distinctive academic programs and encourage nationally recognized faculty to best meet the needs of our educational community.*

Though broadly defined, this mission statement gives a strong signal to faculty and staff of the priorities, strategies, and directions to guide their short-term activities and decisions. While it is comparatively short and easy to read, it clearly delineates four department priorities:

1. high quality (distinctive) academic programs,

2. nationally recognized faculty scholarship,

3. highest quality student graduates, and

4. relationships with the educational community.

These priorities do not suggest appropriate or best priorities for all academic departments. It is, however, an example of the long-term guiding principles important to every department. Recall your "environments" analysis earlier in this chapter and review the strengths and priorities of your institution from Exercise 3.1. Get your department's stakeholders actively involved in this process and review your mission statement specific to your current situation. Use Exercise 3.2 to assist you in this process as you guide the development of scope and priority unique to your department.

Key Department Outcomes

Your mission statement describes the long-term intent and vision of the department. It sets the priorities for daily department effort and decision. But meaningful focus may require more than this overall, broad statement of mission. Identifying and defining specific areas where results are vital to department success (key outcomes) is often neglected, but essential to department unity. Key outcome areas common to academic departments are suggested in the literature and are summarized in Table 3.1 (Bare, 1980; Booth, 1982; Creswell, et.al., 1990; Hengstler, et.al., 1981).

When you identify the five or six key outcomes critical to your department mission, you create a cohesive meaning for your many department activities. For example, one department chair's representative listing of her administrative activities is shown in Table 3.2. This list reflects the many facets of department leadership, but is too cumbersome to give focus. Don't underestimate the importance of your own perspectives as you share your vision of the future.

Exercise 3.2
Mission Statement Worksheet

Note here the three or four priorities for your department that you believe are critical to meet the challenges of your changing environments.

1.

2.

3.

4.

With these priorities in mind, prepare a narrative statement that communicates the excitement and future-orientation of this "vision" to your department.

Department Mission Statement

Table 3.1
Key Outcomes Common to Academic Departments

Student Learning
- national scores
- student evaluations
- skill development
- degree completion
- placement data
- alumni relations
- other notable student achievement

Faculty Achievement
- research activity
- research results
- teaching methodology
- teaching effectiveness
- university service
- community service

Academic Process
- budget information
- budget allocation
- planning system
- student records system
- academic program review
- personnel evaluation and review

Constituent Relations
- potential employers
- student groups
- professional organizations
- community organizations
- state government agencies
- federal government agencies

Department Resources
- effective utilization of current resources
- additional support from the dean
- community partnership programs
- extramural grant funding
- private development funds

Table 3.2
Chair Activities

The following items reflect one department chair's administrative duties and activities recorded chronologically during a given week.

- schedule classes
- seek opportunities to recognize constituent groups
- make service committee assignments
- establish department standards
- review and monitor student achievement
- make regular field visits to important constituents
- assess employer satisfaction with our graduates
- improve lab facilities
- establish acceptance of diversity among faculty
- encourage student participation in programs
- involve faculty in department goals
- coordinate summer school assignments
- generate development funding sources
- seek additional budget resources
- compare national scores and results
- build a cooperative spirit among faculty
- allocate limited resources
- select advisory committees
- invite relevant stakeholders to make campus visits
- approve student course requests
- call and conduct faculty meetings
- set curricular standards
- support student organizations
- hire quality department staff
- invite new class offerings
- interact regularly with advisory committees
- establish department goals
- handle student discipline problems
- assign teaching loads
- submit annual budget
- provide feedback to faculty
- require job descriptions for all positions
- encourage effective classroom learning
- provide adequate research support to faculty
- monitor enrollments
- submit faculty salary recommendations
- counsel students
- advise and counsel faculty

Table 3.3
Chair Activities Within Key Outcome Areas

Student Learning
- encourage effective classroom learning
- review and monitor student achievement
- assess employer satisfaction with our graduates
- encourage student participation in programs
- counsel students
- handle student discipline problems
- support student organizations
- compare national scores and results

Faculty Achievement
- establish acceptance of diversity among faculty
- build a cooperative spirit among faculty
- involve faculty in department goals
- provide adequate research support to faculty
- call and conduct faculty meeting
- provide feedback to faculty
- assign equitable teaching loads
- make service committee assignments
- advise and counsel faculty
- submit faculty salary recommendations

Academic Process
- establish department standards
- establish department goals
- invite new class offerings
- seek additional budget resources
- require job descriptions for all positions
- approve student course requests
- coordinate summer school assignments
- schedule classes
- monitor enrollments

Constituent Relations
- select advisory committees
- interact regularly with your advisory committees
- make regular field visits to important constituents
- invite relevant stakeholders to make campus visits
- seek opportunities to recognize constituent groups

Department Resources
- allocate limited resources
- submit annual budget
- set curricular standards
- improve lab facilities
- generate development funding sources

Suppose this same chair, using information from her department analysis, organized the many "activities" into five key outcome areas critical to department mission. The results of this systematic approach appear in Table 3.3. This not only identifies each area critical to department success, but gives a longer-term focus to and framework for the many daily functions, activities and decisions.

Department Mission and Key Outcomes Statement

Take the time to prepare specific descriptions of the key outcomes important to achieve your department mission. These will interpret and explain the mission statement to all interested parties and greatly enhance the long-term direction, contextual meaning and unity of purpose for the department. What better way to make decisions of priority and time commitment? What better process for encouraging daily activity toward the longer-term goals? Your leadership no longer need focus on fragmented individual activities; but all daily functions, decisions, and activities can now be directed and prioritized in relation to desired end-results or key outcomes.

Look again at the earlier example of the education department chair's mission statement with the inclusion of "key outcomes."

> The mission of the Department of Educational Administration is to establish distinctive academic programs and encourage nationally recognized faculty scholarship. This department's main purpose is to prepare quality student graduates to best meet the needs of our educational community.
>
> We, the faculty and staff of the Department of Educational Administration, do earnestly and consistently strive for:

- *PRIORITY FOCUS ON STUDENTS AS CLIENTS AND COLLEAGUES*

> Student achievement is realized only through a partner relationship and a supportive and collaborative involvement with faculty.
>
> Student graduates will be recognized by the educational community, state constituencies, and alumni groups as the highest quality in the state.

- *DISTINCTION IN RESEARCH AND SCHOLARSHIP*

  Research and scholarship distinction by faculty and students is a measure of the department's ability to compete at the university and national levels.

  Collectively, the faculty will present a portfolio of national scholarship, professional activity, and collegial presentation.

- *EXCELLENCE IN PROGRAM DESIGN AND DELIVERY*

  Selective offerings of academic programs will reflect the opportunities of our educational community and the strengths of our department.

  A fundamental purpose of this department is to achieve recognized excellence in the design and delivery of all offered academic programs.

- *DISTINCTION IN SERVICE TO THE EDUCATIONAL COMMUNITY*

  In order to distinguish the department as a powerful service provider, departmental staff and faculty must be visible and recognized as contributing members of our educational community.

- *ENLARGEMENT OF RESOURCES FOR DEPARTMENT SUPPORT*

  Since excellence is worth the cost, the acquisition of sufficient professional resources within the department is essential for our success.

  Professional grants, constituent support, student funding, and university development activities are valued and encouraged by the department.

This complete mission and key outcomes statement paints a visual challenge of the future for this particular department. Notice how the long-term commitment to excellence in each of the major areas of department accountability is explained and given emphasis. This allows the chair, staff, and faculty to keep their day-to-day discussions, activities, decisions, and goals focused on key outcomes—not merely another long, fragmented list of daily activities.

From your earlier and ongoing analyses, identify and describe the key outcomes critical to your department's future in Exercise 3.3. Specific attention to departmental strengths should give you insight into important outcomes unique to your particular external environments.

Exercise 3.3
Key Outcomes Worksheet

Using your mission statement from Exercise 3.2, list the four or five key outcome areas critical to your department. Consider only major areas that, if neglected, will be detrimental to the department's future.

1.

2.

3.

4.

5.

With these specific areas in mind, prepare brief narrative statements to detail your department's commitment to excellence for each key outcome.

Key Outcome I

Key Outcome II

Key Outcome III

Key Outcome IV

Key Outcome V

The format and wording of your mission statement is not the important issue. Informal, but consistent, communications are sometimes just as effective. The critical issue is to develop your mission and identify the key outcomes with sufficient faculty input, involvement of relevant stakeholders, and your dean's approval. Be certain that your university, your college, your department and your constituents value achievement in each of your identified key outcomes. Once developed, you must share it. Post it in the department, distribute it to clients, publish it in the newsletter, initiate a memo, or include it in your annual "state of the department" correspondence. Figure 3.2 shows an actual letter from one chair attempting to share her department's long-term aspirations (mission and key outcomes).

Figure 3.2
Memorandum

Copy of memo from department chair who was experiencing some lack of "team" attitude among faculty.

TO: Department Faculty

FROM: Department Chair

DATE: February 15, 1993

SUBJECT: Next faculty meeting

In our last faculty meeting, four areas were identified for attention. I would like to detail some specific suggestions under each area. At the upcoming faculty meeting, I would like to discuss: 1) if faculty agree that these four foci are appropriate, and 2) if so, if they agree with the suggestions I have offered under each category and if they have any additional suggestions. Here goes:

1) Integration of the department

We need to think and function as one department. I perceive this objective as a prerequisite to departmental survival. To this aim, I recommend:

...The whole department, not areas within the department, decide on doctoral student admission. Admission of all new doctoral students, beginning immediately, should be considered in light of departmental needs not any one area's needs. We will have an opportunity at the next faculty meeting to recruit doctoral students with departmental welfare in mind.

...Recruitment of new faculty should similarly be viewed as a decision to benefit the whole department and not pit factions within the department against each other. We need to carefully select candidates who can meet the department's research, teaching, and service expectations as well as meet the needs of our external constituencies.

2) Responsive to stakeholder needs

We need to be attentive to our environment and major stakeholders within it (students, alumni, industry, administration). Towards this aim, I propose:

...We need major revision in our curriculum (courses offered, content of the courses, and teaching methodology). We can start this effort with input from our focus groups. We need to get rid of useless courses, be more flexible in teaching methods (e.g., have students do real-life projects and use team-teaching), and draw in more students to our classes rather than require them to take our classes.

...We need to be responsive to administration's concerns. I feel that it is primarily my responsibility as chair to be a boundary spanner and get this information for the department. I will be meeting again with the dean in the next two weeks on these matters. Once I get a clear understanding of administration expectations, then we as a faculty will need to consider the desires and if and how we can meet them.

...We need to rethink our advising. Our block advising consistently results in complaints to the dean's office. I understand our department has more complaints than any other department. There are two major types of complaints: 1) our advisors have a bad attitude (they do not want to do this), and 2) the advisors are poorly trained, (they do not know the technical regulations, do not attend training sessions, do not call the dean's office with questions, and give bad advice). Any suggestions are welcome at this point.

3) Greater visibility for the department

We need to have a higher profile as a department for our research, teaching and service activities. To do this, here are some ideas:

...As I indicated in my earlier memo, this department has an excellent teaching and research record. We need recognition for this. I would like each of you to summarize one of your recent publications, research streams, or research activities into layperson's terms and either directly contact the media or give me that summary. Also highlight your noteworthy teaching accomplishments and service contributions. We will be preparing a media release for the recent focus groups and hope to use these to get into several media outlets.

...We need to serve on more high visibility university committees. If any of you are interested, please let me know. My Committee Manual lists 65 possible choices. Select your committees carefully; some would be killers for untenured faculty. Consult me or other senior faculty before you agree to participate.

4)   External funding

We need to become resource independent from the dean. To this aim:

...We need to develop and cultivate ties with potential donors. I would like faculty to try to develop grants and get monies that support our mission. As chair, I will take a lead role in getting funds and am closely working with the development office now on several projects. Please bring your ideas in this area to our next faculty meeting.

In sum, I see great potential for departmental growth and these are only a few ideas that can take us into a favored departmental position. Please react to these ideas (directly to me if you will not be at the next faculty meeting). I am very open to new ideas.

Effectiveness will not be measured by formality nor method of distribution. When developed collectively, clarified in written form and openly shared (whatever your process), a shared statement of department key outcomes becomes your vehicle for fulfilling the inspirational role of department chair.

Establishing Department Goals

With mission and key outcomes identified and described, you are now ready to set goals. Department goals give direction toward departmental mission, and when tied to key outcomes, give specific initiative to department potential. Most administrators agree that setting specific achievement targets or goals enhances performance toward those goals. However, these same administrators often fail to use any type of formal goal-setting process in their own organizations. While many reasons (or excuses) may be given, they typically include:

- Previous experience with goals which were unclear or difficult to measure.

- A belief that goal-setting requires extra paperwork in addition to the regular administrative responsibilities.

- The misconception that chairs don't have time to formally develop and manage a department goal-setting process.

If these or other rationales describe your opinions preventing you from setting departmental goals, you should rethink your position. An active planning process will impact department unity and enhance department achievement. And besides, what other choices do you have?

An overwhelming number of studies provide specific support for the goal-setting process. One review of the many studies provides impressive evidence that goal-setting improves performance (Latham & Yukl, 1975). Another, independent analysis of over one hundred well-designed field and lab studies from 1969 to 1980 further support the positive relationship between goal-setting and performance (Latham & Steele, 1983). These and other reports form a combined list of over 200 separate studies supporting the strong relationship between goal-setting and productivity (Katzell & Guzzo, 1983).

The basic premise of goal-setting theory seems obvious in its assertion that "the conscious intentions of people influence their actions and behavior." But the real questions are "What actions?" and "To what end?" The conclusions drawn from the many goal-setting studies are not consistent in all dimensions, but several common principles emerge. Setting goals will improve overall organizational performance to the degree that:

- the goals are specific, measurable, and clearly stated;

- the goals are set at high levels of achievement but still remain within the reasonable realms of attainment;

- regular attention and feedback is provided; and

- each goal is related to key organization outcomes.

Your Department Goals

Mission and key outcomes give unity and inspire excellence. Goal statements, on the other hand, focus on the shorter term (usually annual) planned activities that operationalize your plan. By tying each department goal to one or more key outcomes, you are defining the measurable achievements of highest value to your department and college. Simply stated, department goals express, in writing, which accomplishments are important this year to you, your faculty and your dean. Thus, department goals must be clearly stated, challenging, and achievable during the planning year.

As discussed earlier, you should review your department goals to see if they:

- are measurable and specific,

- are challenging, yet achievable,

- provide feedback to individuals, and

- are directly related to your key outcomes.

Examples of department goals related to each suggested key outcome are shown in Table 3.4. These reflect the level of specificity and measurability needed to make them effective.

Table 3.4
Sample Goals Related to Key Outcomes

Student Learning

1. Increase the ratio of students completing their degree programs to at least 80% by the end of the year.

2. Develop a department system to track all graduates and keep record of their placement and work data for a five-year period following graduation.

3. Organize a faculty task team to analyze, revise, and update the department measures of student achievement.

Faculty Achievement

4. Increase the number of top-tier faculty publications in the department by 15% each year for the next five years.

5. Appoint a faculty task team to review all undergraduate curricula with a recommendation by year's end to streamline current offerings on the basis of relevance, student demand, and employer interests.

6. Improve the overall department teacher effectiveness rating to an average of 3.00 (on a 4.00 scale) and reduce the number of ratings below minimum (2.00) to less than 10% of all teacher ratings.

Academic Process

7. Initiate a formal faculty planning system within the department to be ready for implementation at the beginning of the next academic year.

8. Work with the dean and staff to develop a better data base of budget information for monitoring, evaluating, and projecting department budgets.

9. Automate all student records within the next three years. Develop a new system that would allow PhD records to be automated by the end of this year, all graduate records by the second year, and to include all student records by year three.

Constituent Relations

10. Identify and develop an advocate relationship with the director (or key staff) of the Federal Science Foundation. (This is not a goal of the chair, but for the department as a whole.)

11. Initiate an employer advisory board (or increase the number of members on the current advisory board).

12. Improve department visibility to field constituents by raising the number of field contacts to at least 25 each month. These will be coordinated through the department secretary.

Department Resources

13. Increase the amount of planned giving from department constituents by 50% of last year's totals.

14. Hire a new staff member before the end of summer to provide grant preparation support to faculty.

15. Initiate a partnership consulting program with the local Chamber of Commerce.

Building a strong relationship between department goals (short-term) and identified key outcomes (long-term) provides an emotional unity and inspirational sense of direction to your department. Review the key outcomes specified in your department mission and use Exercise 3.4 to consider one or two measurable goals for each key outcome.

Exercise 3.4
Department Goals Worksheet

Your mission and key outcomes statement provides a long-term orientation to the future.

Your department goals, on the other hand, must focus on planned achievements for the coming year. Before preparing your department's goals, review your analyses and examine each of your stated key outcomes from Exercise 3.3. For each key outcome, prepare a written goal of measurable achievement for this year. These goals may not reach the final, long-term success hoped for in each area, but will initiate department effort in the right direction.

Key Outcome # I:

| *Goal #* | *Goal Statement* |

| *Goal #* | *Goal Statement* |

| *Goal #* | *Goal Statement* |

Key Outcome # II:

| *Goal #* | *Goal Statement* |

| *Goal #* | *Goal Statement* |

Goal #   *Goal Statement*

Key Outcome # III:

Goal #   *Goal Statement*

Goal #   *Goal Statement*

Goal #   *Goal Statement*

Key Outcome # IV:

Goal #   *Goal Statement*

Goal #   *Goal Statement*

Goal #   *Goal Statement*

Key Outcome # V:

Goal #   *Goal Statement*

Goal #   *Goal Statement*

Goal #   *Goal Statement*

Additional suggestions for setting measurable goals can be gleaned from the literature and are included here as ideas from which to build your own set of department goals.

- *Student Learning:* standardized score levels, student evaluations, admission ratios, placement data, program completion ratios, individual knowledge and skill development levels, alumni accomplishments, diversity of student body, etc.

- *Faculty Achievement:* department publication record, faculty evaluation levels, department record of grants and grant proposals, student/faculty ratios, national recognition by discipline, relevance of academic programs, faculty/student relations, department teaching quality, etc.

- *Academic Process:* department goal-setting process, program evaluation systems, chair evaluations, levels of faculty involvement, department resource allocation and budget priorities, faculty collegiality, department diversity, etc.

- *Constituent Relations:* coordination with other departments, activity with other colleges, relationships with government agencies, involvement with employer groups, membership in professional associations, etc.

- *Department Resources:* resource utilization, department results and outcome measures, college and university resources allocations, grants, partnerships, private funding, etc.

Department success is not accomplished simply by providing written statements of direction and intent. Effectively sharing this vision with your staff and faculty in relation to accomplishing change and effecting results are quite different matters. To do this, chairs must involve others and motivate individual activity toward the accomplishment of department goals. This challenge is addressed in Chapter Four.

4

DEPARTMENT RESULTS: GOAL SETTING AND ACTION PLANNING

I find the great thing in this world is not where we stand,
but in what direction we are moving.
— *Oliver Wendell Holmes*

You've completed your department analysis, prepared your mission and key outcomes statement and identified this year's department goals. As your initial department planning meeting comes to a close, you hand out your department plan and deliver an impassioned plea for faculty support and involvement. Your faculty respond with enthusiasm, excitedly place the new planning document into their briefcases—and complacently head back to their separate offices and individual interests.

The call for leadership discussed in Chapter One is not a rhetorical imperative. Integrating your department plan into the lives of faculty and staff requires communication and action. This is what breathes life into the department leadership model. To personalize this challenge, ask yourself two questions:

1. With you as chair, will your department achieve more than it would have otherwise?

2. How do you plan to influence your department's future?

Lieberson and O'Connor (1972) proposed that organizational success is impacted more by its external environments than its managers. This may not seem surprising since organizational success is defined as the organization's responsiveness to its environmental conditions and changes. But effective chairs do more than react and adapt to their environments. Several more recent studies support leadership as the primary force in organizational performance. This is particularly true when leaders (proactive) are distinguished from managers (reactive) (House & Baetz, 1979; Smith, Carson & Alexander, 1984; Weiner & Mahoney, 1981). Your implementation skills and practices will make a difference to the future of your department.

The department leadership model (Figure 4.1) places the implementation process in perspective as it addresses the question, "How do you plan to get there?" Effective implementation involves staff and faculty through individual goal setting and action planning.

IMPLEMENTATION: HOW DO YOU PLAN TO GET THERE?

As you anticipate your involvement with individual staff and faculty, don't forget the challenge discussed in Chapter Two: to develop collective team attitudes. This department team attitude begins with you. As you interact with your faculty, always keep your focus and attention on:

- guiding their activities and decisions toward department mission and department goals,
- encouraging individual performance goals and personal achievement, and
- creating enjoyable relationships.

Effective team climate not only adds value, but makes it a better place to work. You don't need everyone to agree, but mutual respect and good humor is imperative. Life is simply too short to do otherwise.

Influencing department personnel is a two-dimensional leadership skill: (a) influencing your support staff and (b) influencing your faculty. Most faculty are interested in "rational explanation of purpose" and "support from colleagues." On the other hand, your support staff are most influenced with a show of "confidence and support through effective delegation" (Keys & Case, 1990).

Figure 4.1
Department Leadership Model: Implementation

Department Analysis

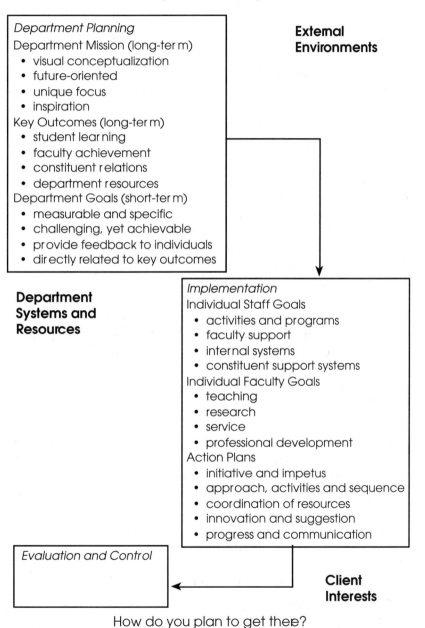

How do you plan to get there?

These differences derive at least in part from the professional stature of faculty. Since faculty members are colleagues as well as experts in their respective disciplines, they typically expect to be more involved in departmental goal setting and decision-making. In contrast, your support staff are more directly responsible for the department's programs and activities. Determining your appropriate or desired leadership style will not be the same for your staff as for your faculty. Don't expect it to be either simple or easy, but you'll need to decide how much to involve each of them in "setting" and "implementing" department goals.

Involvement in setting goals (participation) and the details to accomplish them (directiveness) are two parts of the same question that must be considered separately (Muczyk and Reimann, 1987). Understanding the importance of this difference is a critical first step in building collective team attitudes. Your faculty and staff have different skills, abilities and needs. You will find different reasons at different times for inviting participation in goal setting. You will experience differing times and places to direct specific activities to accomplish goals.

Consider for example, that your department decided to limit the number of majors offered and create a new major in a growing field. Staff participation in this decision may not be necessary since it requires the expertise of the discipline, but faculty involvement (participation) is critical. Once the decision has been made and approved, however, your support staff will likely be the ones to make the programs and activities work (directiveness). These are separate, but important leadership choices in the implementation process.

As you involve faculty and staff, your challenge is to determine their appropriate level of "participation" in setting department goals before deciding how much "directiveness" is appropriate in determining how to accomplish those goals. Leaving the discussion of action planning (directiveness) to the next section, turn your attention now to encouraging individual goal setting compatible with your department's goals.

Individual Goals: Your Support Staff

Department goals give impetus and encourage activity, but are difficult for staff members to take full responsibility. Setting individual goals with and for your staff is one of your best ways to communicate departmental direction. Take some time to share with them not only what the mission and goals are, but how they as individuals will be involved. Develop goals that assign individual accountability to each staff member.

How many staff do you have reporting to you at this time? What are their job duties and responsibilities? Have you sufficiently communicated to them the department mission, key outcomes, and annual goals? Do they understand their specific responsibilities in achieving department goals? While these seem to be obvious questions, the answers may surprise you. Staff involvement, effort and contribution toward departmental goals are essential. But don't forget our earlier assertion that staff are best influenced by recognizing their achievements and specifically delegating their responsibilities. Support staff exist to provide general support to your department. Therefore, their individual goals must be set to specifically direct their activities toward the broader department goals. In relation to each of the department's key outcomes, individual staff goals will focus on:

- activities and programs to support student learning,
- support for faculty achievement,
- internal systems to improve academic process, and
- support systems to build constituent relationships.

Not all staff members will need to set individual goals for each department goal. But you must provide the direction to see that they are set when needed. Review your department goals and determine which ones require individual staff assistance. Whether your staff members develop their own goals with your input or you establish them with staff input, it is important to state them clearly and in writing. Some input from staff is always wise in setting individual goals. However, it may be counter-productive to encourage full participation when department systems are already determined or when you have already established department goals. Staff autonomy, involvement, and personal growth will come more from allowing them to decide how to best accomplish their goals (directiveness) than from pretending to allow them to set their own goals (participation). Understanding the difference between participation (what is to be done) and directiveness (how it is to be done) is critical to effective delegation. An open dialogue of this difference will contribute to better staff relationships and will be discussed in detail in the action planning section of this chapter.

Of course, individual staff goals must be prepared with actual target measures (percentages, amounts, numbers, deadlines, etc.) and must clearly specify the support and resources needed. Examples of individual objectives compatible with department goals are shown in Table 4.1.

Table 4.1
Staff Accountabilities: Examples for Consideration

Department Goals	Staff Focus	Examples for Consideration
Student Outcomes	Activities and Programs	• improved record systems • innovative alumni tracking • surveys and analyses • informational reports • student diversity identification • lab support • advising programs
Faculty Achievement	Faculty Support	• clerical support • word processing support • research support • grant proposal support • feedback systems • instructional support
Academic Process	Internal Systems	• computer assistance • technical training • program evaluation • budget information • internal communication • facilities maintenance
Constituent Relations	Constituent Support Systems	• media coverage • advisory board planning • networking information • development programs • stakeholder analysis • public relations and clientele rapport

Review your department goals from Chapter Three and identify which of your current staff can or should be directly included. Propose individual goal statements (that assign individual staff responsibilities) for each department goal you judge to be required.

These, of course, are seldom written without staff input and discussion, but keep in mind that the purpose of this process is to assign individual staff accountability (delegation) for measurable results. Make these assignments clearly but encourage your staff to use their initiative to decide how to carry out the assignment. The "how to" portion of delegation will be addressed in depth in the action planning section. Recall the discussions of Chapter Three as you prepare these individual goal statements and review the degree to which they: (a) are specific, measurable, and clearly stated; (b) are set at high levels of achievement but still remain within the reasonable realms of individual attainment; (c) are directly related to department goals; and (d) establish accountability for and provide feedback to the individual.

Individual Goals: Your Faculty

As you review your department goals, ask yourself who will accomplish these goals? They cannot be accomplished alone. Your staff will assist you as discussed, but only to the degree that their efforts are appropriately directed (delegated) and to the extent they have the required academic expertise. Achieving department goals requires the expertise and knowledge of your faculty. Your leadership challenge is to actively involve your faculty in the implementation process by having them set their own individual goals.

Involving faculty, however, is a delicate process. While department mission and success are certainly desirable achievements for all concerned, chairs must remind themselves that individual faculty goals always take first priority. And that is the way it should be. Universities and academic departments widely report three basic categories of faculty outcomes: *teaching, research* and *service*. These categories continue today as a viable guide for encouraging specific goals with each faculty member.

These three dimensions, you'll notice, are all closely related to your departmental key outcomes and this connection is the key to influencing individual faculty goals. Your efforts in this area must not be directed toward establishing equal goals for each faculty, but in "balancing" individual faculty goals toward the overall department goals and outcomes. As with any organizational effort, the key to success lies in making individual faculty goals compatible with department goals.

While department goals may (by necessity) be initiated by the chair, individual faculty goals must be developed and determined by the faculty themselves. Thus, the role of department chair is not to develop annual goals for faculty members, but to share a vision of the future with their faculty and encourage, excite, or inspire them to develop individual goals in relation to this departmental mission. Regular discussion with each faculty member is both desirable and necessary as you involve your faculty. Discuss department directions with your faculty and lead them to develop their own individual goals (in writing) to:

- encourage personal growth and development,
- identify challenging results to be achieved during the coming year, and
- relate their efforts to department goals and key outcomes.

Remember, individual faculty goals must also meet the criteria of measurability, clarity, challenge, attainability, and feedback-orientation. Most importantly, this process provides a vehicle for you to discuss individual faculty effort and achievement. What better way to encourage faculty activity than to focus on their faculty-initiated individual goals? Faculty planning will vary by department as well as by the particular chair and faculty member involved. Your departmental faculty planning guide should identify the three or four "key outcomes" from your mission statement (teaching, research, service) and specify observable measures in each are important to faculty evaluation. A sample listing is included here, for illustrative purposes only, with possible measures to consider in each of the three basic categories of faculty outcomes:

Teaching
- student evaluations
- student learning
- course load

- class size
- class projects and independent study
- new course development

Research
- number and type of publications
- number and type of papers presented
- number of grant proposals
- grant acceptances
- ongoing streams of research
- research activity with other faculty and other universities

Service
- student advising/counseling
- college or university committee assignments
- department programs or assignments
- professional memberships or positions
- approved consulting activity
- personal development activity

If you are developing this form for your own individual goals, add at least one additional category of "professional development" that specifies growth in each of the department chair roles discussed in Chapter One: manager, leader, faculty developer and scholar. Exercise 4.1 contains an example of one department's "Faculty Planning Guide." Use this, revise it, or create your own with measurable parameters as deemed appropriate.

As discussed earlier, the professional status of faculty implies that "participation" or initiative is essential in establishing faculty individual goals. Thus, your individual "Faculty Planning Guide" is an excellent vehicle to influence faculty focus and effort. Encourage your faculty to develop challenging goals from their own strengths that will contribute (when combined with other faculty's goals) to overall department success. This provides an excellent opportunity to enjoy your faculty. Discuss faculty member contributions, recognize individual accomplishments, and encourage change or improvement as you build your collective team.

Exercise 4.1
Faculty Planning Guide

Department of: _____

Name of faculty member: _____

I. TEACHING

A   Formal Instruction:

Course	Number of Students	Student Ratings
_____	_____	_____
_____	_____	_____
_____	_____	_____

New Courses Developed _____

_____

_____

_____

B.   Informal Instruction:

1.   Student Advising:

# of undergraduate advisees _____

# of masters advisees _____

# of doctoral advisees _____

2.   Project, Thesis, Dissertation (if applicable):

students with independent study projects _____

masters students at thesis stage _____

doctoral students at dissertation stage _____

List your students who will be completing thesis or dissertation this year _____

3.   Other: _____

_____

_____

II. RESEARCH/SCHOLARLY ACTIVITY

A.   Focus of Scholarship (research stream): _____

_____

_____

_____

B.   Manuscripts (planned or in process books, monographs, articles and papers):

Title	Intended Audience or Journal	Planned Completion Date
_____	_____	_____
_____	_____	_____
_____	_____	_____

C.   Grants, Grant Proposals, or Other Development Projects:

Title	Source of Support	Planned or Submitted
_____	_____	_____
_____	_____	_____
_____	_____	_____

D.   Presentations:

	Subject/Title	Place/Audience	Planned Date
1. Original or Keynote:	_____	_____	_____
2. Secondary:	_____	_____	_____

III. SERVICE

A.   Department/College:

_____

_____

B.   University:

_____

_____

C.   State/Regional:

_____

_____

D.   National/International:

_____

_____

IV. PROFESSIONAL DEVELOPMENT PLANS

_____

_____

ACTION PLANNING TO MOTIVATE INDIVIDUALS

To this point, the discussion has focused on the development of individual faculty and staff goals to give impetus to department goals. This section turns now to the other half of the delegation question—directiveness.

Clearly, goal achievement will not just happen. It requires definitive action and individual effort. Many sources have defined "action planning" as the process to initiate such effort and activity (Drucker, 1974; Pearce & Robinson, 1989; Randolph & Posner, 1988; Steiner, 1979; Yavitz & Newman, 1982). In simple terms, action plans state the specific and sequential activities needed to accomplish a given goal or objective. They further identify the individual responsible for each activity and the specific time frame within which each step will be completed. Action planning forms (as shown in Figure 4.2) are available in most formalized management programs and are both common and self-explanatory in nature.

Quite often, especially in professional organizations, action planning is misunderstood and frequently misused. When action plans are required by the system, they tend to create additional work for individuals, add non-productive activity, and initiate directive leadership by default. Action planning must not be a system requirement. Action planning needs to be an available, but self-selected option. Our discussions of "participation" in setting goals and "directiveness" in accomplishing goals emphasized that neither process is inherently good or bad, but that they are different. Participation focuses on "what" we should be doing and raises the question of "who" should determine it. Directiveness, on the other hand, is the question of "how" the established goals can best be accomplished (action planning). By separating these issues, it becomes easier to understand and discuss the primary roles of the chair, faculty, and staff within the department.

- *Chairs* provide long-term department direction (mission, outcomes and goals).

- *Faculty* contribute academic expertise and participate in defining mission and setting goals.

- *Support staff* report more directly to the chair and become more involved in the action planning process.

Figure 4.2
Action Planning Form

Individual Goal Statement: _____

_____

_____

_____

_____

Action Plan to Accomplish Above Goal:

Specific Action Steps	*Planned Completion Date*	*Person Accountable For This Step*
1.		
2.		
3.		
4.		
5.		
6.		
7.		
8.		

Action planning is a valuable planning and management tool. Action plans provide sequence and accountability to support staff but can be equally beneficial, at times, to faculty and department chairs. Action planning provides five significant benefits: (1) initiative and impetus; (2) approach, activities and sequence; (3) coordination and resources; (4) innovation and suggestion, and (5) progress and communication. These represent benefits to the individual, but each will also accrue value to the department.

1. *Initiative and Impetus.* Action planning helps individuals find a starting point and gives impetus to their annual goals.

   A staff member assigned the goal of expanding the department's available lab space may have a good general idea of what is required, but not be too sure of which comes first—the room, equipment, a demand study, funding sources, or faculty agreement. Preparing an action plan (refer to Figure 4.2) not only approves the actual first step, but also adds impetus by actively including others in the process .

2. *Approach, Activities and Sequence.* Action planning determines the specific steps, proper sequence and appropriate time frame of activities to best accomplish a given goal.

   Newer faculty members determined to upgrade the quality of their research publications may not know the best way to approach this task. But by developing an action plan, the initial development steps, identification of journal options, co-authorship potentials, colleague review panels, as well as specific writing schedules, can be more clearly identified.

3. *Coordination of Resources.* Action planning provides a vehicle to coordinate effort, access resources, and involve other individuals as necessary to achieve selected goals.

   Chairs faced with the difficult and complex goal of revising the department curriculum may greatly benefit from an action plan detailing the steps, time frames and accountabilities required. Involving staff, faculty, or other administrators is facilitated by knowing not only who, but what and when their participation is desired.

4. *Innovation and Suggestion.* Action planning allows individuals to solicit ideas and suggestions on how to approach difficult goals or goals that they have not yet experienced.

Faculty challenged to improve their teaching might not be open to critique or suggestion from others, but may be willing to seek such assistance in the process of developing an action plan at their own initiative.

Action plans for individuals can accomplish great things when encouraged judiciously, but are usually self defeating when required by the system.

5. *Progress and Communication.* Action planning allows individuals to communicate progress toward goals that may otherwise be difficult to evaluate.

A staff goal to automate student records may need some method of interim reporting. If the new record system will not be operational until its completion, it may tend to frustrate individuals who need more frequent feedback. Action plans report specific and significant progress in each action step without waiting for final goal achievement.

Notice that all of the benefits listed are for the individual, not the department. Action planning is for individuals. Benefits to the department are, and must remain secondary. Action plans are not helpful for all department goals nor for all individual goals, and become burdensome or even useless when attempted for all goals. Action plans are, however, extremely valuable to the staff employee, faculty member, or department chair who is faced with particularly difficult, new, or complex goals.

Your challenge is to decide when action plans will assist rather than hinder individual performance. Developing written action plans initiates activity toward goal achievement, gives organization to individual ideas, and invites innovation into the planning process.

Faculty Action Planning

Faculty goals are best developed by faculty. Action planning for faculty can be suggested and encouraged, but should be developed or reviewed only by invitation of the faculty member.

Your influence, when used wisely, can be significant in this individual goal setting process. But the decision of "how" to accomplish these individual goals is best left to the discretion of each faculty member. Suggest the action planning process to your faculty only when they want help in getting a new direction started or need help in accomplishing difficult aspirations. However, if no particular difficulties are indicated, there is little need to discuss or even see their implementation plans. You can assist, support, and suggest faculty action planning, but to be effective, action plans must remain a faculty prerogative.

Action Plans for Support Staff

Staff performance, on the other hand, requires more direct input as they initiate activity toward department goals. But even with staff, action planning should be done by the staff employee whenever possible. The decision of how much direction is required or appropriate depends on the skills, experience, and initiative of the staff member. As you review staff progress on individual goals, ask for action plans only for those goals not being accomplished. Action plans for routine or achievable goals will not improve goal performance. And even for more complex goals, have your staff develop their own action plans with input and assistance only as needed. Action plans developed by your staff should be reviewed, but not collected. *The action plan is for the individual—not the department.* With the realization that you are managing individuals, make a conscious determination of both when and if to review individual action plans. Assess the value of developing action plans and determine how prepared the individuals are to create their own.

Use the action plan form to identify one of your department goals that might be difficult to accomplish or that is particularly important to your dean and develop an action plan for achieving that goal. Include the following steps as you prepare your action plan:

1. *Summarize* all major activities (action steps) that you can anticipate as important to the objective. This will organize the process in your mind and also prevent the appearance of inactivity.

2. Indicate the planned or expected *completion* date of each action step to coordinate effort and to encourage action within an acceptable time frame.

3. *Specify* who will be accountable for the completion of each action step. Notice that some of the steps in your action plan may very well become individual goals for your staff. Also note that if coordination is needed with the dean's office, other departments or external constituents, this action plan presents an excellent vehicle for communicating those support needs.

Remember, action plans should be developed by the individual. This exercise is *your* action plan for *your* goal. This will help you explain to staff or faculty how they can prepare their own action plans, but it does not imply that you should develop action plans for anyone except yourself.

Action planning should not be perceived as a burden or unwelcome additional assignment. Action plans are for the individual staff, faculty, or chair to initiate, organize, coordinate, innovate, and communicate progress toward their own individual goals. While it may not be productive (in most cases) to require or even to review someone's action plans, encouraging individuals to develop their own is always beneficial. Action planning is indeed a vehicle for implementing department plans.

Action plans are for the sole purpose of supporting activity toward individual goal accomplishment. Individual action plans are for individuals and are to be used by individuals to:

- decide how and when to begin,

- determine the approach and sequence of activities,

- coordinate resources and other people,

- invite innovation and suggestion, and

- communicate specific and interim progress more effectively.

As department chair, you should suggest, coach, or require action plans for each individual staff and faculty member in your department as you judge necessary. By using action plans to encourage and assist individual performance, you will find it an excellent tool for training staff, guiding faculty and strengthening department unity. Department relationships will be more enjoyable and long-term department direction easier to influence.

EVALUATION AND CONTROL:
HOW WELL ARE YOU DOING?

Since this chapter is titled "Department Results," it seems reasonable to conclude with a discussion of *evaluation* and *control*. The term "control" should not mean a monitoring or checking up on daily activities and assignments. The purpose of control should be instead to help individuals become more productive in accomplishing personal goals and contributing to the achievement of department success. Specifically, the evaluation and control process should:

- recognize individual achievement and contribution to department mission and key outcomes,

- encourage individual goal performance specifically in relation to department goals, and

- suggest, assist or require the development of individual action plans in areas identified for emphasis, planning or improvement.

Figure 4.3 presents the full department leadership model showing the evaluation and control component as the integrating link between department activity (implementation) and department mission (planning).

Control is best explained in the context of planning and implementation. Without planning and implementation, there is nothing to evaluate. The question of "Where do you want to be?" must precede the question of "How well are you doing?" When goal setting and action planning are included with their focus on "How you plan to get there," they provide a vehicle for not only monitoring how well you are doing, but for initiating progress in that direction.

You will influence department goals to the degree you impact individual goal performance. Take care not to evaluate activities or programs as an end in themselves. Review them rather in terms of how they contribute to individual goals and a unified department effort. While you must effectively and consistently share department direction, encouraging individual goals and assessing progress toward them demands supportive consultation through the evaluation process.

The control process is not just a monitoring of activities nor an evaluation of performance, but a recognition and encouragement

Figure 4.3
Department Leadership Model: Evaluation and Control

Department Analysis

Department Planning

Department Mission (long-term)
- visual conceptualization
- future-oriented
- unique focus
- inspiration

Key Outcomes (long-term)
- student learning
- faculty achievement
- constituent relations
- department resources

Department Goals (short-term)
- measurable and specific
- challenging, yet achievable
- provide feedback to individuals
- directly related to key outcomes

**External
Environments**

**Department
Systems and
Resources**

Implementation

Individual Staff Goals
- activities and programs
- faculty support
- internal systems
- constituent support systems

Individual Faculty Goals
- teaching
- research
- service
- professional development

Action Plans
- initiative and impetus
- approach, activities and sequence
- coordination of resources
- innovation and suggestion
- progress and communication

Evaluation and Control

Long-Term Department Success
- mission statement
- key outcomes
- department goals

Individual Goal Achievement
- staff goals
- faculty goals

Action Plans
- interim progress
- initiation of activity
- individual development

**Client
Interests**

How well are you doing?

of individual planning and development. The control process includes the annual review, but requires more frequent and informal discussions to be meaningful. As you prepare to inspire your staff and faculty to greater productivity, plan to meet with them informally and often to enjoy these interactions and to unify their efforts toward department goals. An effective evaluation process will include three priorities.

1. *Long-Term Department Success.* Consistently and continuously focus on your mission and key outcomes statement. This is the "single mindedness" so important to effective leaders. Whether with your staff or faculty, your first priority is to assess progress toward each of your stated key outcomes.

   These discussions need not be lengthy nor overly detailed, but are valuable for two reasons. First, they set the direction or basis for developing your department goals, and second they encourage meaningful feedback to you and your staff concerning those goals.

2. *Individual Goal Achievement.* For department key outcomes judged as not succeeding, your priority becomes one of more directly evaluating achievement of individual goals. When the desired, long-term department results are not being reached, the achievement of individual goals becomes your best measure of contributions toward those goals.

   As you evaluate progress toward individual goals, examine the value and appropriateness of these goals to the individual and to the department. This invites communication concerning individual and department goal compatibility from their point of view.

3. *Action Planning.* If individual goals are not being achieved, the final step in the control process is to evaluate specific activity toward achieving them. Don't fall into the activity trap of valuing the achievement of action plans as ends unto themselves. Assessing action plan achievement is only an interim measure of progress toward individual goal achievement.

This process allows you to discuss, coach and initiate activity toward individual and department results. Your discussions will likely be different for staff than for faculty, and they will certainly vary depending on the individual. Your "faculty planning guide" can be an excellent tool for influencing your faculty through the evaluation (control) process. The question of how well your department is doing becomes a more productive discussion when approached simultaneously with the preceding question of how you plan to get it there.

Refer back to your department mission and key outcomes statement and revisit your planned departmental goals. Your environmental analysis from Chapter Three will give you a feeling of the appropriateness and acceptability of these departmental aspirations as you consider the individual goals of your staff and faculty. How can you specifically influence your faculty with the faculty planning guide? How might you more productively direct your staff through the action planning process? The control process for you may simply be the decision of which goals for faculty and which action plans for staff merit your attention. Take this opportunity to use your judgment, your imagination, and your leadership skills. Listen carefully as you discuss goal direction, goal achievement, and specific action planning efforts.

CONCLUSION

Your challenge as department chair is to build a collective team attitude that strengthens relationships and encourages long-term department success. Inspire your staff and faculty to develop and accomplish individual goals that, when combined, will support the department mission. Don't make your control activities just additional steps in the sequence of department management. Integrate them into your leadership plan for the future (department planning) and inspire your faculty and staff (implementation) toward that potential (evaluation and control). Remember, it is your department, your future, and your decision; so consider it, attend to it and enjoy it.

Part III

Enhancing Personal Productivity

Part III, the remaining chapters of this book, discuss the skills critical to effective department leadership. Chapter Five explores the important issues of time management. It redefines the concept of "team" effectiveness and the use of time from the chair's perspective. Chapter Six introduces the skills of managing conflict through recognizing, responding, and resolving interpersonal differences. Chapters Seven and Eight conclude with methods for reducing stress and for developing yourself both personally and professionally.

5

MANAGING TIME: FOR DEPARTMENT CHAIRS ONLY

> *"I didn't have enough time to get it all done." "There just aren't enough hours in the day any more." "The week is almost over and I haven't yet found the time to start my top priority project." "If I want this job done right, I'll have to do it myself." "I guess this project will have to be mine because it's just too important to assign to a faculty member." "I'll assign this project to a staff member just as soon as I get it off and running."*
>
> *Need more hours in the day? Yes, but that's out of our control. Every person gets exactly the same number of hours each day. It is more productive to examine sources within your own control. Procrastination. Fear of offending. Ego. Pride in your own abilities. Lack of delegation. Misplaced priorities. Desire to please. Resolving these issues promises to improve the time problems of department chairs.*

From autonomy, scholarship, independence, and individualism to accountability, administravia, social interaction, and accessibility; this is the transition from faculty to chair discussed in Chapter One. This transition typically represents an addition of responsibilities rather than a substitution of existing responsibilities. Newly appointed department chairs are faced with the need to continue their professional achievements while significantly increasing their service or administrative workload, all with the same amount of time available.

Time has always been, and likely will continue to be, a problem for department chairs. But trying to find more time is neither prudent nor productive. The old cliche holds true, "It's not how much time you have that matters, but what you do with the time you have." Time becomes problematic for department chairs as (1) their stress levels increase from the added responsibilities and (2) they make choices that decrease the time available for their personal and professional interests. From our recent survey of over 1,000 department chairs, the top five items reported as contributing most to their stress levels were:

1. inability to keep current in the discipline or to find time to publish,

2. insufficient departmental resources,

3. participating in work-related activities outside regular working hours which conflict with personal activities,

4. evaluation of and interaction with department faculty, and

5. unrealistic self-expectations.

All five top stressors are related to the department chair's time problem. Seeking resources and interacting with faculty are heavy time users which often result in taking time away from the chair's professional and personal activities. And it is the unrealistic expectations that chairs create for themselves to perform effectively and to continue the research of their discipline that exacerbates the time problem.

TIME: THE PROBLEM

Another survey of over a hundred department chairs indicated that the majority of their time was spent "preparing reports, budgets, etc." and in "interaction with faculty" (Meredith & Wunsch, 1991). The least amount of time was reported as being spent doing "scholarly research," "professional study and reading within their discipline," and in "personal or social interactions." Time was not the problem. The lack of time for personal and professional growth activities is the continuing problem for department chairs.

A common theme from administrators and managers alike is the problem of "not enough time or too many things to do in the time available." In many existing time management seminars, the emphasis is on identifying "time wasters" and then managing priorities to reduce or avoid these nonproductive activities. There is much agreement that budgets, reports, correspondence, and other paperwork is a major consumer of department chair time. Unplanned interruptions (visitors and telephone) and too many unnecessary meetings are also universally reported as major time wasters. While it is always good advice to reduce or avoid such wasters of your time, this alone seldom addresses the real time problem. As department chair, your problem is not to find more time, not to find less to do, nor even to spend less time on nonproductive time wasters. The real time problem of department chairs is to confront the real issue: gaining more control of your activities, your aspirations, and your time.

TIME: THE ISSUE

Terry Adams, the newly appointed chair in a department of anthropology has just spent the entire afternoon trying to resolve a serious scheduling problem brought to light by the department scheduling secretary.

The majority of Terry's previous week was spent preparing an unplanned revision of the budget report for central administration and resolving an unexpected disagreement between two faculty members.

Two weeks prior, Terry was approached by a government agency requesting on-site visits with the entire faculty. Thus, this week has been spent in a series of meetings with department faculty and several university administrators.

And yesterday, Terry was called in for an unscheduled work meeting with the dean to discuss the status of the curriculum review committee.

In each of these instances, the problem is not what the new department chair is doing, but *who* is in control of what is being done. In all three cases, someone else is determining *what* to do and *when* it must be done.

Of course, in none of the above cases can the chair refuse to cooperate or attempt to resolve the problems. But for the sake of their own time problems, chairs must gain some control of both the content (what) and the timing (when) of their activities. This is the paradox of time management versus department management. As department chair, you need to maintain good working relations with your dean, faculty and staff, but these are the very people who are most often the source of your time problem.

Consider the following sources vying for control of your time:

- Your dean (the boss)
- Your staff (subordinates)
- Your colleagues and other stakeholders (the system).

While each of these are in some part outside of your direct influence, it becomes your challenge as department chair to increase the amount of "self-controlled" time at your disposal. In the first case above, it was a "subordinate" or staff member that was prompting both the "what" and "when" of Terry Adam's time. In the second and third situations where Terry was required to file the budget report and then deal with faculty, it was the system (colleagues, administrators & stakeholders) that determined how the chair was spending time. And in the last instance, the "boss" or dean was in control of what and when the chair was doing. Time management requires you to think about your use of time, not only in the sense of what you spend your time doing, but more importantly in terms of *who* determines what you do and when you do it. The options for gaining more control of your time will be discussed later in this section, but it is important to first identify the real issue of time management—who controls the *content* and *timing* of your activities as department chair?

Department chairs may allow others to exercise control over their activities for various reasons. Chief among these reasons is the (often unconscious) unwillingness to make unpopular or difficult choices. At times, the lack of decision may seem like the best way to maintain an important relationship. In most situations, however, the absence of choice results not only in straining the relationship in the long run, but also in losing control of the timing and content of your job.

For example, if only one additional faculty position has been funded for the coming year and you have two faculty groups vying for that position, postponing the decision is not likely to strengthen faculty relationships and is quite likely to increase and prolong the continuing interruptions from both faculty groups.

On the other hand, a reasoned decision shared with both faculty groups, while surely the more difficult choice, is certain to maintain more control of when and what you will be doing in relation to this problem.

The *problem* of time is the stress of non-productive activity and the lack of time to devote to your own personal and professional development. The *issue* of time management is the question of control. How can you prevent others from controlling the timing and content of your job? How can you gain the control to spend your time more productively both in terms of what you do and when you will do it? Your control as department chair emerges as you set clear priorities and as you make clear (though often difficult) choices in relation to those priorities.

TIME: THE SOLUTION

If the problem is what you do and when you do things in the time available, and if the issue is who controls what you do and when you do it, then the solution must lie in how to gain more *control* over the timing and content of your job as department chair. However, this time management challenge requires the effective use of your time as you gain this control. Gaining control over the timing and content of your job and using this time effectively, includes four areas most directly influenced by your decisions:

1. Unplanned and unexpected *interruptions* from students, staff, colleagues, administrators, or other stakeholders.

2. Formal *meetings*, planned or unplanned, again with any of the above constituents.

3. Discussion, evaluation, and other *interactions* with staff and faculty.

4. *Personal* decision.

Unplanned Interruptions

There is much written, discussed and understood about the problems of unscheduled visits and phone calls. How can chairs gain more control of these interruptions and still maintain working relationships with those who are so willing to take this time? While delegation is often cited as the key to many of your time management problems, two concepts seem more directly related to this particular issue: first, the recognition of your management team or your "management molecule" and second, the specific assignments for responsibility of the next action step or the frequently quoted "monkey on your back" analogy (Oncken & Wass, 1974). Rather than envisioning your role as managing downward to your staff and faculty, consider the role of department chair as the center of your management molecule with the dean above, the staff below, the faculty and other administrators on one side, and your external constituents on the other (see Figure 5.1). This adds some new dimensions to your role of department chair. In addition to the traditional perception of managing staff, now are added the concerns for building relationships with colleagues, establishing networks with stakeholders, and managing your relationship with the dean.

Visualizing your role as the center of this management team also changes your perspective of control. In addition to determining or controlling the activities of your staff, your role now includes directly influencing relationships with your colleagues

Figure 5.1
Your Management Team

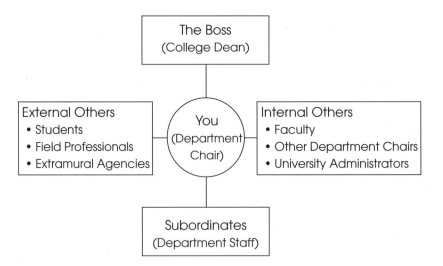

and other administrators, initiating stakeholder networks, and exerting more control (as possible) over interactions with your dean.

The second concept (the monkey on the back) becomes a helpful analogy in gaining more control of your time and activities in relation to those on your management team. Instead of asking who has the "monkeys" on their backs, it is more instructive to discuss the concept of who has the "next move." Each next move is not to be confused with the delegation question of who has the task accountability or project authority, but who will need to take the next action step. Too often a task is delegated but then the "next step" is retained and the delegated task still takes the time and effort of the delegator.

Faced with the first situation, Terry Adams made the choice of getting immediately involved in the scheduling problem. This resulted in a solution, but at the expense of Terry's unplanned time and effort. In this case, it was probably an issue of delegation as well as who had the next move. Regardless of the delegation question, Terry's first reaction would more profitably have been to determine who should be taking the next action step. If the next move were judged to be identifying what information was needed to best determine options and alternatives available, then this "next move" or series of next moves could be assigned to the staff scheduler. This would better utilize the staff member's time and talents and also allow Terry to choose both the when and what of the chair's involvement.

Under the second set of circumstances, Terry chose to prepare the budget and play the role of mediator between the two faculty members. Again, the solution to both of these problems will likely require several "next moves." Rather than simply prepare the budget report, it may have been possible to ask for additional information, examples, and so forth from the budget office or finance officer and even request assistance from university staff in completing the report. And, with the two faculty members, it might prove productive to request each of them to prepare a position statement to be shared prior to any mediation. In both cases you'll notice Terry can give the "next action step" to the other person. This approach enhances the probability of effective solution and equally important, the chair has chosen a significant position of control in the "what and when" of time to be expended.

In the third example, the chair was being pressured by external constituents. This is not pressure to avoid since these groups are critical to the support and success of the department. But Terry's reaction was an effort to maintain a relationship by taking additional unplanned time. How much more control could have been maintained by anticipating this need and inviting the extramural constituent for a planned visit at the department's convenience? Even at this late date, however, Terry might reduce the immediacy of the time commitment by taking the "next move" and asking for time to prepare a departmental report and re-scheduling these visits for a later time when he can be more available.

The fourth case, between Terry and the dean, seems more problematic in gaining some control. And in fact the process of gaining control may surprise you. When dealing with a person above you in the organizational hierarchy, your intent should be to take the next move if you can. As long as you are expected to contribute to the process and as long as the boss has the next move, you do not have control. Therefore, in this case, Terry might determine that the "next move" is to prepare a written report for the dean's input and approval as a recommendation to the full department faculty. While this may at first seem like the chair is taking on additional responsibilities, in fact the dean is relinquishing some control of the timing and content of that assignment.

Interruptions will never be eliminated. They may not even be noticeably reduced. Nor will the problem of interruptions be solved by delegating more effectively. But, by consciously determining for every interruption, what the "next move" should be and then choosing who should take that next move, your time from those many interruptions can be reduced, better managed, and, more importantly, brought within your own realm of control.

Rather than simply identifying your time wasters and listing how your time is now being spent each day, focus your attention on:

1. Who is making the decision of how you spend your time?

2. What impact does your use of time have on your management team?

3. Are you placing the "next moves" where they belong?

Review the concept of your "management molecule" in Figure 5.1 and specifically consider who is on your management team. With this in mind, recall an unexpected interruption you have experienced during the last few days and identify where it fits on your management molecule. Interruptions from persons not on your molecule should not be given significant time from your busy schedule.

Recount this experience and identify who controlled the timing and content of your reaction to that interruption. Using Exercise 5.1, identify what the "next action to be taken" was and who should have taken it. Then, generate several alternatives for taking the "next move" if it was from the dean or external others or for giving the "next move" to a faculty or staff member. This process can prove useful for any future unplanned interruptions you may encounter.

Remember, this is not a process of delegation, it is simply a method to gain more control of what you do and when you will do it. Delegation remains an important issue but often will not

---

Exercise 5.1
Taking Control of Interruptions (Worksheet)

Description of interruption (who, when, why):

Likely impact on Management Team:

  Boss (the dean)
  Internal Others (faculty, chairs, administrators)
  External Others (students, professionals, constituents)
  Subordinates (staff)

What immediate action or actions should be taken as a result of the above interruption?

To gain control of the timing and content of your involvement, who should take the next action step?

If you have determined that *you* should take the next action step, list here some possible ways to keep the responsibility for the "next move."

If, on the other hand, you decide to assign the next action step to the interrupting party, list your options here for placing this responsibility with them and still preserving the relationship.

solve your time problems. You must consciously attend to "who should have the next action step" and your alternatives for getting this next move assigned to the right person.

Formal Meetings

Note what managers, directors, and other administrators have to say about the necessity and value of meetings. "That there are too many, with the wrong people, and are poorly run; that they last too long and that nothing gets followed up. The average manager spends ten hours a week in meetings, and 90 percent of managers say that half of their meeting time is wasted. In some meeting-prone fields like education, the total is much higher" (Mackenzie, 1990, p.136). Department chairs have meetings—lots of them. Your challenge is to make your meetings more effective and consciously reduce the number of other meetings you attend.

Reducing the number of meetings you attend outside your department is relatively easy. Easy, but not automatic. Simply by making a conscious choice each time you are invited to attend another meeting can significantly assist you in this endeavor. One helpful guide is to consider whether or not attendance at a given meeting is "on your management molecule." Will it make a difference to those on your management team? If you are invited to attend a university meeting that will not impact your dean (the boss), your department (staff subordinates), faculty or university colleagues (internal others), or other department stakeholders (external others), then you should decline the opportunity. Even when the invited meetings involve persons on your management team, you should specifically determine: (1) the purpose of and the participants invited to the meeting, (2) your role in the meeting's agenda, and (3) the time and duration of the meeting. And you should determine these in advance of accepting the invitation to attend.

Your decision can then be based on the value of your time in relation to the purpose of the meeting and your relationship to the other attendees. You must also decide whether the length of the meeting is acceptable to the meeting purpose and your relationship to those invited. And finally, you can determine in advance and give proper notice to attend only that portion of the meeting that is pertinent to you or your management team. With these few, simple, but far from automatic decisions, your time spent in other's meetings can be drastically reduced. The choice is yours.

For your own department meetings, you have three choices that can greatly decrease the amount of unproductive time required of both you and your faculty. First, decide whether or not the meeting should be held. What is your intent or purpose of calling this meeting? Specifically determine whether your purpose is to share or exchange needed information, to build relationships with or motivate those in attendance, or to make decisions, either problem-solving or new project related. Once you have specifically defined the purpose of the meeting, then ask yourself if a meeting is really the best way to accomplish this purpose. Can it be achieved satisfactorily with a memo or a phone call to all participants? Is the meeting scheduled more from tradition or habit? Is it actually necessary to get everyone together or could individual information be conveyed more selectively? From this analysis, you may decide that some meetings are not really necessary.

Second, establish the length of time needed for each meeting to accomplish your stated purpose. A beginning and an ending time should be communicated to all invited to attend and then that schedule should be adhered to rigidly. An agenda should be prepared in advance and shared with all participants with time limits for each topic and required decisions noted. One helpful tip is to officially designate one person to be your "timekeeper" and another to be your "recorder." These two simple assignments will pay great dividends as you or others call upon the official timekeeper to keep the meeting within stated time limits and ask the official recorder to note assignments given and to keep the group discussion "on task." This official designation allows you to make such adjustments in a non-threatening and impersonal manner, maintaining group relationships while focusing on the task and holding to the scheduled time limits.

Third, carefully select those persons who should attend each meeting. Inviting everyone so you won't offend anyone usually results in offending several who are invited without their wanting or needing to be there. As you consider who should be invited, the Vroom-Yetton participative decision-making model may be helpful (Vroom & Jago, 1988). According to this model, the decision of who to invite to a meeting should be based on four factors: 1) whether or not the final outcome is important to the department; 2) how much information is needed in the meeting and who has access to that information; 3) whether or not meeting together is necessary to build understanding and acceptance of the outcomes; and 4) if conflict or significant disagreement is likely to be encountered among group members.

As you decide who should attend a given meeting, ask yourself these questions:

1. *Is the outcome of this meeting important to the department?* If your answer is "not really", then the meeting likely should not be scheduled.

2. *Is additional information needed and who has access to that information?* If your answer is yes, then try to anticipate who has the information and be sure they are invited participants. If you already have the needed information or if some in your department have no access to the data, then a meeting (at least for those individuals) may not be productive.

3. *Are those to be influenced by the outcome of this meeting likely to understand and accept the solution and value of the decision?* If their understanding and acceptance is likely, then the decision to hold the meeting can be determined mainly from your information needs. However, if the answer to this question is no, then you may need to hold a meeting even if additional information is not needed. Such group interactions can, and should if needed, serve to form group consensus or at least an appreciation for the concerns at hand.

4. *Is there likely to be significant disagreement among participants in method or outcome decisions?* If conflict is likely, then a meeting with those involved will be helpful. As will be discussed in Chapter Six, bringing up differences when all parties are present is an important first step in resolving those differences.

However, when differences do exist, if all parties do not have the department's interests in mind, a meeting, while helpful, must not be for the purpose of a group decision. Discussion is important and necessary to resolve disagreements, but when individuals have differing self-interests, the chair should clearly maintain the final decision.

Thus, a few conscious choices prior to holding your meetings will allow you to reduce the number of department meetings without adverse impact, shorten the length of meeting times to save additional nonproductive time, and be more selective in determining who to invite. Inviting only the right people and for the right reasons will result in less wasted time for yourself and your faculty. Exercise 5.2 is intended not to develop agendas for more effective meetings, but to reduce the number of meetings you choose to attend outside of your department. It will also emphasize your ability to choose when a department meeting will be productive and to choose the appropriate participants for each meeting. Identify one external meeting that you have recently attended or plan to attend in the near future. Using the checklist provided, determine if you should have or if you will attend the external meeting and, if so, which portion of it.

Exercise 5.2
Choosing Meetings (Worksheet)

External meeting to be considered:

Relationship of this meeting and its invited participants to your Management Team:

    Boss (the dean):
    Internal Others (faculty, chairs, administrators)
    External Others (students, professionals, constituents)
    Subordinates (staff)

Stated meeting purpose:

Your specific role or purpose in attending this meeting:

Based on the above considerations, list your decision to attend and note the time, duration, and schedule that are worth your time and commitment:

    Attend full meeting
    Attend part of meeting
    Not attend this meeting

Consciously asking these simple questions prior to your decision to attend each external meeting can save you significant time without loss of necessary information and important contacts.

Now identify a meeting planned within your own department. With the directions in Exercise 5.3, review the purpose and participants invited. On this form, indicate the proper duration of such a meeting and identify the appropriate participants to be invited.

Exercise 5.3
Departmental Meeting Planning Form

Identify purpose of meeting:

Question #1: How important are the decisions or outcomes of this meeting to those on your management team?

After considering this question, do you still want to schedule this meeting? _____ Yes _____ No

Question #2: Do you have sufficient information for the purpose of this meeting and do you know who has the needed information?

If you have the necessary information, you may want to handle this one with a memo or individual phone calls.

If you need additional information, who are those on your management team that are likely to have useful data? Indicate those here as participants.

Question #3: Are those on your management team likely to understand and accept the decision or other outcomes from this meeting without participating? _____ Yes _____ No

If not, you will want to include all members of your team whose understanding and acceptance is particularly important.

Question #4: Are there likely to be differing opinions among those on your management team? _____ Yes _____ No

If so, list those here as participants

Based on the above considerations, note below those members of your management team to invite to this meeting.

For more productive sessions, conscious effort should be made to invite only those included for the above reasons rather than always inviting everyone.

Faculty/Staff Interactions

It is not a problem to spend time with your faculty and staff. In fact, this is your most vital role. Don't try to eliminate or even reduce these interactions. Your staff and faculty are the very essence of your job. Reducing your time problem does not require less interaction, but it does require you to gain more control of unplanned interruptions and reduce your nonproductive meeting time. The best advice to be given for improving your interactions with faculty and staff is to welcome it, enjoy it, and focus it on the goals and mission of your department. Whether you are evaluating performance, resolving differences, providing motivation and direction, or soliciting ideas and suggestions, follow the examples discussed in Chapters Two, Three and Four. Your departmental interactions need not be reduced, but they can be made more cohesive and productive as you allow individual achievement and encourage personal action plans toward your department mission and identified key outcomes. To better enjoy your time with staff and faculty, be sure to establish and communicate a clear department mission. Take some time to identify the key outcomes for your department mission and develop short-term goals toward those outcomes. Then, rather than many multi-directional and fragmented discussions, you will be more able to unify your intent and evaluation of all faculty and staff interactions. Such a review of the information and exercises in Part II is your best guide to improving departmental interactions.

Personal Decision

The first step in resolving your time problems, perhaps the only step really required, is to recognize and accept the fact that *you* are the problem and the solution. Time management is really a misnomer. Time is a constant. Every day has the same number of hours for every individual and the amount of time available cannot be managed. What can be managed, however, is what you choose to do and when you choose to do it.

Consider the following example. A graduate student in business administration recently complained of a severe time problem. She was failing one class and performing below average in two others. Her specific complaint was that she simply did not have enough time to succeed in all three classes. A brief discussion revealed that the real problem was a fiancé who had just moved into the area resulting in a lack of personal time for that relationship. An interesting solution was suggested by the student. While she seemed to be unable to control her busy time schedule, she asked if her professor would help gain this control. She voluntarily prepared herself a strict daily study schedule and asked if it might be posted publicly. She then checked in every day with the professor to enforce her adherence to the schedule.

No more time was made available, no one else changed their behavior, but the results were significant. Grades in all three classes rose to above average and sufficient time with the fiancé was still available. While this student wasn't initially able to take control of her time problem, she did take the initiative to gain assistance in retaking some control. Control, not time, is the problem. Your choices make the difference. As in this case, if you can't seem to get control in some areas, create a system or other external assistance to help you regain needed control. Even in this instance the choice remained with the individual.

It is not uncommon for department chairs to incur serious demands on their time as a result of taking on too many additional responsibilities and then blaming those activities for their time problems. Mackenzie stated that this problem often occurs "because we simply do not know what to say in difficult situations. So we end up saying yes when we didn't want to, we allow other people to interrupt us because we don't want to offend them, we accept confusing instructions from the boss because we don't want to appear stupid...and we end up falling further and further behind" (Mackenzie, 1990). The problem, the issues, the solution is not more time—it is more control of what you choose to do and when you choose to do it.

Department chairs cannot, must not, place the blame for their time problems on other factors or other persons. Such an external focus implies that the control lies elsewhere. With this perception, there is no solution. Recognize that only as you take personal responsibility for your time problems can you make the necessary choices to resolve them.

6

MANAGING CONFLICT CREATIVELY: VALUING DIVERSE PERSPECTIVES

L *ouis Whythe was hired as an associate professor with a strong research record and having been tenured at another university. That was 13 years ago and there was absolutely no reason to believe there would be any problems with his teaching or other professional duties. However, every time Dr. Whythe teaches, disaster strikes. Irate students and the dean demand that he must not be allowed to teach again. Other department chairs say they will not send their students to the department for courses students need. The department is saddled with an unpleasant, unresponsive, bitter, but potentially able faculty member who also manages to make every committee meeting unpleasant through his combative nature. He has not received a merit increase in several years and has made an appointment to see you about this year's annual review. How will you handle the meeting? Do you know what his true interests are in academe? Can you make a productive situation out of your upcoming confrontation meeting?*
(Washington State University Department Chair Workshop)

INTRODUCTION

In the above case, professional growth and change cannot be made without conflict. Nothing is as important for American higher education than the emergence of academic leaders equipped to handle conflict.

A study conducted by the Center for the Study of the Department Chair found, not surprisingly, that chairs identified conflict with colleagues as their major source of stress. As noted in Table 6.1, over 40 percent of the department chairs suffered excessive stress from "making decisions affecting others, resolving collegial differences and evaluating faculty performance" (Gmelch and Burns, 1991). In contrast, only 17 percent of the chairs complained of excessive stress from resolving differences with deans and 5 percent with students. Thus, chairs suffered from more interpersonal conflict with their colleagues than with their deans or students. Overall, no other chair activities produced as much stress as these faculty-based responsibilities.

Table 6.1
Chair Confrontational Stressors

Making decisions affecting others	45%
Resolving collegial differences	45%
Evaluating faculty performance	42%
Resolving differences with superiors	17%
Resolving differences with students	5%

Source: Center for the Study of the Department Chair Survey, Washington State University and UCEA, 1990.

CONFLICT AND DEPARTMENT CHAIR DISSATISFACTION

In the study, chairs also described when they felt most dissatisfied with their jobs. Second only to bureaucratic red tape and paperwork was the chairs' frustration with interpersonal conflict. Sixty percent of their dissatisfaction came from dealing with faculty involved with the following sources of faculty conflict.

1. *Inter-Faculty Conflict.* Most of the chairs' dissatisfaction came from faculty disagreeing with each other which resulted in "bickering, whining, and feuding," "acting without reason," and "ideological and personal wars."

2. *Faculty Attitude.* Chairs felt disappointed when faculty were seen as "unimaginative, apathetic, disengaged" colleagues, who "are recalcitrant and no longer focused on the mission" and "do not measure up to their potential."

3. *Unsupportive Faculty.* Another source of conflict surfaced when faculty did not support the direction of the department, e.g. "chairs dealing with faculty resistance to improvements and change," "faculty acting unreasonably (and selfishly), thereby causing turmoil and compromising the achievement of departmental objectives," and "when interpersonal differences between faculty inhibit the mission of the department and...basically work against the good of the department."

4. *Unsupportive Chair.* Chairs also expressed remorse when they could not support their faculty and had "to make decisions which cause great disappointment to my colleagues," and "when I can't, or don't, have the resources to reward good faculty."

5. *Role of Evaluation.* Although evaluation is inherent in their role, chairs reported difficulty in having to "evaluate their colleagues," "conduct annual reviews," "make tough decisions on merit evaluations and salaries," and "fire faculty."

6. *Role of Mediation.* Finally, the chairs' role in mediating conflict between their colleagues caused them dissatisfaction. One chair expressed concern over "severe faculty confrontations" and another expressed difficulty "when I have to referee bad interpersonal relations between faculty."

The remaining 40 percent of conflict situations causing chair dissatisfaction stemmed from dealing with higher level administration. Chairs commented about the "frustration from lack of support" or "unresponsiveness from higher administration," and "when higher-up administrators do not share information upon which decisions affecting my department are made." Another concern came from chair's frustration when "higher administration requires what seems to be excessive paperwork" or "unrealistic deadlines" and "requesting reports that are never responded to." Finally, chairs felt conflict with higher level administrators when they had opposing values, felt unappreciated for the work that has been done or successes accomplished, and when their recommendations or input were not accepted.

All these forces place department chairs in a difficult position. In order to foresee and respond effectively to crises and pressures, chairs need to be equipped with creative conflict management skills. This chapter focuses on the skills necessary to help chairs recognize, respond to and resolve conflicts within academe.

APPROACHES TO CONFLICT MANAGEMENT

When you think of conflict what is the first word that comes to mind? Most chairs develop images of controversy, disagreement, or differing opinions between faculty members. While negative images of conflict may predominate, controversy is not necessarily undesirable. Emotional responses to conflict may be positive (excitement, enjoyment, stimulation, curiosity, creativity, commitment, involvement), negative (anger, distrust, resentment, fear, rejection), or even neutral (change or a different point of view).

No matter what your answer or reaction, one of management's main functions is to adjudicate conflicting demands (Katz and Kahn, 1978). How should you as department chair view conflict within your department? The answer rests in your basic philosophical approach. As Table 6.2 portrays, three philosophies reflect managerial attitudes toward conflict: traditional, behavioral and principled. The first two philosophies espouse views historically held in the management literature (Robbins, 1974) and the third proposes a new way to handle conflict.

Table 6.2
Approaches to Organizational Conflict

Period	Philosophy	Nature	Prescription Strategy
1890s - 1940s	Traditional	Destructive	Eliminate
1950s - 1980s	Behavioral	Natural	Accept
Present	Principled	Necessary	Encourage

Traditional

The traditionalists' approach from the late nineteenth century through the middle 1940s was simple: Conflict is destructive and therefore should be eliminated. The role of the manager was to purge conflict from the organization. In higher education, the traditionalist chair believed that conflict should be thoroughly analyzed, suppressed, and eliminated—it was destructive and should be avoided (Williams, 1985). Naturally, exceptions to this generalization existed, but the bottom line seemed to be that conflict created ill dispositions rather than constructive dialogue.

Behavioral

By the 1950s, the behavioral view gained attention in the literature and in practice. Freud believed that aggressiveness was an innate, independent, instinctual disposition of people. Therefore, we should accept conflict as natural and inevitable, since "complex organizations, by their very nature, have built-in conflicts. Disagreements over goals clearly exist. Sections compete for recognitions. Departments compete for prestige....All compete for power" (Robbins, 1974, p. 13). As management guru Warren Bennis points out: "Conflicts stem basically from differences among persons and groups. Elimination of conflict would mean the elimination of such differences. The goal of conflict management is, for us, better conceived as the acceptance and enhancement of differences among persons and groups..." (Bennis, Benne, and Chin, 1969, p. 152). Since it is inevitable, then, the department chair's strategy should be to manage conflict. However, just managing conflict because it is inevitable does not go far enough. In order to tap the real benefit of conflict, it should at times be promoted to explore common grounds, interests and mutual benefits—thus, leading to the third approach to conflict management.

Principled

By the 1980s, management of conflict entered into what has been termed a principled approach. Principled conflict management promotes integrity and high standards in the resolution of disputes such that both parties exhibit righteous, upright and trustworthy principles in attempting to satisfy mutual differences. The use of "tricky tactics" gave way to a more honest, open, principled approach. In essence, this approach views conflict as a necessary and encouraged condition of administration. It promotes diverse perspectives in the hope of finding new, creative solutions. In the 1970s, a review of managerial practices found few administrators employing principled philosophy (Robbins, 1974). Over the past decade, however, successful administrators have begun to recognize that in many instances conflict can be a sign of a healthy academic organization. The recent popularity of the Harvard Negotiation Project (Fisher and Ury, 1983) has influenced even a broader-based use of principled conflict resolution.

This chapter presents and discusses the necessary ingredients for principled resolution. The three R's of principled conflict management (Recognize, Respond and Resolve), are presented here with the following objectives in mind:

1. *Recognize* the nature and causes of conflict;

2. Identify and explore effective *response* options; and

3. Practice the art of principled conflict *resolution*.

CONFLICT RECOGNITION

Your first step toward a positive and constructive conflict management style is to recognize the nature and causes of conflict in your department and the university or college. Unfortunately most people take conflict personally and believe that if they are involved in controversy it must be due to their personality. As Allan Tucker (1992) points out, some chairs feel that for some reason conflict is their fault. However, even though chairs may not like to talk about conflict, they need to accept the idea that it occurs. Ironically, conflict in complex organizations such as universities and colleges is sewn into the institutional fabric.

A review of the research on organizational conflict reveals ten structural relationships which actually create conflict among faculty and administrators, regardless of who is involved. It is important to recognize these role and organizational characteristics and not take the tension and conflict personally. Rather, understand that such conditions are built into the university, college and department structures.

Take a moment to answer the ten questions in Exercise 6.1 to assess more specifically the nature of conflict in your department and institution. Remember, not all conflict is negative and unnecessary.

Exercise 6.1
Department Chair Working Conditions

Instructions: Indicate the extent to which each of the following conditions exist within your current department or college/university.

1. Organizational Structure

relatively flat organization	1	2	3	4	5	6	7	formal hierarchy (6-7 levels)

2. Degree of Authority

informal/ autonomy	1	2	3	4	5	6	7	routinization and rules & regulation

3. Degree of Specialization:

low job specialization	1	2	3	4	5	6	7	high job specialization

4. Staff Composition:

homogeneous faculty & staff	1	2	3	4	5	6	7	heterogeneous faculty & staff

5. Managerial Supervision:

loose/autonomous supervision	1	2	3	4	5	6	7	close supervision

6. Departmental Decision Making:

democratic	1	2	3	4	5	6	7	autocratic

7. Source of Power:

personal power	1	2	3	4	5	6	7	positional power

8. Reward and Recognition:

abundant rewards and resources	1	2	3	4	5	6	7	limited rewards and resources

9. Interdependence Among Work Units:

autonomous independent units	1	2	3	4	5	6	7	interconnected dependent units

10. Roles and Responsibilities:

faculty-oriented	1	2	3	4	5	6	7	administration-oriented

Scoring

Total your score from the exercise and compare it to the suggested conflict quotient below.

50–70	High conflict
30–49	Moderate conflict
10–29	Low conflict
0–9	Minimal conflict

To gain insight into your answers, and the inherent nature of conflict in colleges and universities, the following ten summaries of the research explain the basis of the questions in Exercise 6.1.

1. *Levels.* Most would agree that as the size of an organization increases, goals become less clear, interpersonal relationships become more formal, departments become more specialized and the potential for conflict intensifies. These assumptions have been supported by research in educational organizations. Specifically, Corwin (1969) found that 83 percent of the schools with six or seven levels of authority reported high rates of disagreement between faculty and administrators as contrasted to 14 percent in schools with three or fewer levels of authority. Not unexpectedly, as the administrative line-authority in universities increases, the potential for conflict between the echelons also increases. How many levels can you count in your university or college? Even more important, what do you perceive to be the psychological and sociological distance between each level—in other words, how high is your hierarchy, both in levels and psychological distance?

2. *Rules and Regulations.* Generally, as job structure increases, the amount of role certainty increases, thus reducing *inter*-personal conflict between employees. However, with greater job structure, employees also feel greater *intra*personal role conflict since they become confined by routinization, rules and regulations. In higher education, where faculty have a great deal of autonomy, the potential for interpersonal conflict increases since roles and expectations become less clear and more difficult to monitor and supervise. On the flip side, this autonomy also reduces their potential intrapersonal conflict. Are you and your faculty governed by tight rules and regulations and job definitions? If so you can expect less interpersonal conflict with your colleagues, but greater conflict within individuals with fewer places to go and grow.

3. *Degree of Specialization.* In a study of schools, high degrees of specialization increased the level of conflict intensity. Therefore, secondary schools segmented into departments suffer more conflict than homogeneous elementary schools. Higher education institutions with departments housed in separate buildings experience more conflict than secondary schools.

This, of course, does not presuppose that elementary schools represent a more positive working environment than colleges; conflict can also cause positive outcomes. Nevertheless, are the departments within your college highly specialized and relatively autonomous? If so you may find them in competition for common resources and in conflict with each other.

4. *Staff Composition.* Established groups have been found to develop more constructive conflict than ad hoc committees (Hall and Williams, 1966). Therefore one would expect high staff turnover to stimulate conflict within organizations (Robbins, 1974). Given that faculty tend to be less mobile in higher education than other professions, their stability may be a factor in reduced departmental conflicts. What proportion of your faculty are tenured and stable? You should consider not only longevity but differences in age, gender, background, values, and other demographic and psycho-social factors which influence interpersonal conflict. For example, as both age and tenure increase among staff members, the degree of conflict decreases. While a homogeneous staff may experience less interpersonal conflict than a heterogeneous group, the conflict generated from the diversity of the mixed group may result in productive and healthy changes. If you have an established, homogeneous faculty you may have less conflict than more diverse departments—but are your faculty meetings challenging and productive?

5. *Nature of Supervision.* The closer one is supervised the more conflict will be created. While this may be true, what is the desired outcome of the close supervision? If change is required in employee behavior, then close supervision may be necessary and lead to positive results. Faculty in higher education plan and control their own work and work style, and as long as they produce the desired results in teaching, research and service, close supervision may create unnecessary tension. Do you give your productive faculty the supportive autonomy they need, and the struggling faculty more guidance?

6. *Participation in Decision-Making.* Faculty assume involvement in departmental decision-making. Interestingly, as the level of participation increases, the amount of conflict also increases. Most studies support the conclusion that participation in

decision-making and conflict are positively correlated. This is especially true where value differences exist, as will be noted in the resolution section of this chapter. The assumption behind participatory decision-making is that the quality of the decisions will increase with more input. While this may be true in most cases, there are definitely tradeoffs among time, efficiency and effectiveness.

7. *Sources of Power.* French and Raven (1968) suggest five bases of social power. In essence, department chairs can influence faculty through several sources: through the authority vested in the position (legitimate power); through their ability to provide rewards and recognition (reward power) or punishment and withholding rewards (coercive power); through their knowledge and skills (expertise power); and/or through personal persuasion (referent power). Summaries of research indicate that the use of expertise and referent power (personal sources) yields greater satisfaction and performance of the staff than coercive power (Yukl, 1981). Normative organizations such as universities and colleges rely predominantly on symbols rather than coercion or financial reward to influence employees. Leaders in these organizations, department chairs in particular, use informal control by virtue of both their personality and position to motivate and coordinate their colleagues (Etzioni, 1964). In fact, "low and moderate levels of power...can assist in improving coordination and, therefore, work to reduce conflict. But where power is excessive, as perceived by a less powerful group, one may expect it to be challenged, causing increased conflict" (Robbins, 1974, p. 48).

In higher education, faculty hold exceptional power due to their professionalism; their expertise critically contributes to the success or failure of the department. You, as chair, must recognize these sources of power and use them wisely. Power decisions should be made on the basis of department productivity, not on the expectations of conflict.

8. *Rewards and Recognition.* Rewards and recognition also contribute significantly to conflict. When a differential reward structure is used for two or more groups or departments, conflict is likely to occur. In other words, the more rewards emphasize

separate performance rather than combined performance, the greater the conflict (Walton and Dutton, 1969). This is even more prevalent if the groups perceive they are competing for the same or limited resources. If you must divide a fixed sum of merit increases among your faculty, you will likely encounter conflict between and among colleagues.

9. *Interdependence.* In much the same way that differentiated reward and recognition create conflict, the more faculty must rely on each other, or one department rely on another department, or one academic course builds on another to complete a task or gain achievement, the more conflict will increase. In his definitive work on conflict, sociologist Georg Simmel (1955) concludes that conflict will occur when the activities of one individual or group have a direct consequence on another's ability to achieve its goal.

10. *Roles and Responsibilities.* Managers, who perform liaison or linkage roles in organizations, often find themselves in role conflict situations (Kahn et al. 1964). Academic department chairs encounter even greater role conflict since they are in a somewhat unique position without common management parallels. Researchers have found that department chairs are plagued with inherent structural conflict since they must act as the conduit of information and policy between the administration and the faculty of the institution (Lee, 1985; Milstein, 1987). The ambiguity and role conflict results from attempting to bridge the administration and academic cores of the university, which are organized and operated differently (Bare, 1986). The academic core of teaching and research operates freely and independently in a loosely-coupled system, whereas the managerial core maintains the mechanistic qualities of a tightly-coupled system. Therefore you are at the heart of the tension between the two systems. While this dynamic conflict between administration and academics is critical in order to maintain higher education organizations, it does place you in a difficult position to mediate between your demands and the faculty's. You may feel trapped between the pressure to perform both as a faculty member and as an administrator. These pressures unique to departmental chairs result in a paradoxical dilemma to fill a Janus

position (referring to the Greek god with two faces), both as a faculty member and an administrator.

In summary, a review of the research in educational institutions reveals ten work relationships which inevitably increase the intensity of conflict among colleagues. It is not difficult to infer that higher education institutions are potentially plagued with conflict due to their many levels, rules and regulations, specialized disciplines, heterogeneous staffing, participatory decision-making, segmented rewards, high interdependence, use of authoritative positional power, and tension between the academic and administrative core of faculty and administration.

The purpose of recognizing the nature of conflict in this section is not to debate whether the conflict from these organizational characteristics is negative or positive, but for you to recognize that conflict exists, that it need not be avoided, and that it not to be taken personally. You then need to *respond* appropriately when it arises—the subject of the second R of conflict management. As chair, you need to realize that regardless of the causes, how you respond to these conflict situations is your personal responsibility.

CONFLICT RESPONSE

Having identified the nature and causes of conflict in your department, now devote your attention to the options you have to respond to these conflict situations. The pioneering work of Kenneth W. Thomas (1976) provides a theoretical construct and a human relations instrument to test the practical application of individuals' response options (Thomas & Kilmann, 1974). Basically, think of your response options as organized along two behavioral dimensions: (1) how *assertive* you are in terms of trying to satisfy your own concerns and interests, and (2) how *cooperative* you are in terms of satisfying the interests and concerns of others. The strength and weakness along these two dimensions form five conflict response styles, as displayed in Figure 6.1. Much of the following discussion is based on the original work of Thomas and Kilmann (1974) and is adapted, for sake of illustration, to the potential conflict between department chairs and faculty.

Figure 6.1
Conflict Management

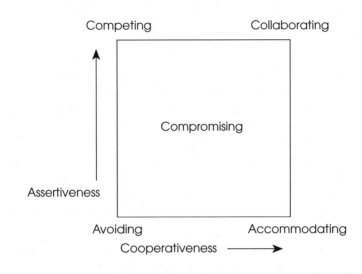

Competition (High Assertiveness and Low Cooperativeness). In this response style you would choose to pursue your own or your department's interests at the expense of staff or faculty. This is a power-oriented mode in which all power sources (both positional and personal), would be used. It requires you to use your ability of persuasion, academic rank, position, or reward and punishment to win.

Accommodation (Low Assertiveness and High Cooperativeness). The opposite of competition is accommodation where neglect of your own or the department's concerns may be necessary to satisfy faculty needs. This self-sacrifice response may take the form of yielding to faculty points of view, of giving personal time to promote needs of faculty, or of being altruistic in dealing with faculty concerns.

Avoidance (Low Assertiveness and Low Cooperativeness). In the event you choose not to address issues and neither assert nor cooperate, you are avoiding confrontation. You may choose this response to sidestep an issue, postpone it until later, or withdraw from it completely.

Compromise (Intermediate Assertiveness and Cooperativeness). The choice of a compromise response style seeks an immediate, mutually acceptable solution which partially satisfies you and your faculty. Rather than striving for the best solution, compromise centers on the resolution of conflict by splitting the difference, exchanging resources, or seeking a middle position response.

Collaboration (High Assertiveness and High Cooperativeness). Collaboration represents the ideal response to conflict between you and your faculty. Given time and cooperation, you can work together to satisfy your own interests and concerns, as well as those of your department and faculty. But, as you are well aware, it does require time and cooperation.

Before addressing resolution, several points should be made about conflict responses. First, seldom is a single option chosen, in fact often a blend of all five response styles may be used to achieve the final resolution. Second, collaboration is not always the most effective and efficient response style. It takes time and the willingness of all to engage in collaborative response styles. And finally, many advantages and disadvantages can be attributed to each response style in varying situations.

The question is not what is the best style, but when is it advantageous for you to use each of them. Figure 6.2 outlines the advantages and disadvantages of each conflict style. Competition is useful when you need quick action and when protection is needed against faculty who take advantage of nonassertive behavior. You may wish to accommodate when an issue is of little importance to you or when it is important to build relationships with faculty. Avoidance may be useful when you believe the risk clearly outweighs the gain or when more information is needed. When an expedient solution is needed in order to resolve time pressure, compromise may be your best temporary solution. Finally, you should include your faculty in a collaborative effort when an issue is too important to compromise or when new, permanent solutions are required.

Figure 6.2
Selecting Appropriate Conflict Responses

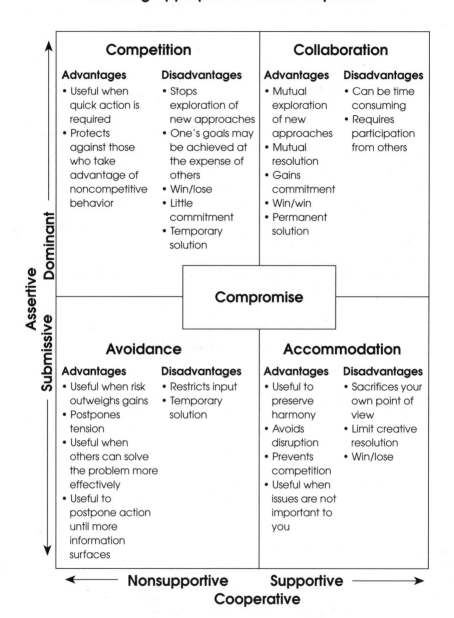

In summary, the effectiveness of a response style depends on the conditions of the conflict situation. One style is not always better than another, but you should select the best response to match the situation, taking into consideration the advantages and disadvantages of each style. Chairs and faculty should have enough flexibility, skill and comfort to use any of the five styles. Rather than discuss style preference, you need to assess which style produces the desired resolution and builds the desired relationships.

The framework of Thomas and Kilmann can be extended by asking two basic questions: (1) Is the *substantive outcome* very important to the manager? and (2) Is the *relationship outcome* very important to the manager? These two questions can help you decide which style best suits your needs. The outcome question relates to "assertiveness" on the vertical axis in Figure 6.1 (importance of outcome) and the relationship question for cooperativeness on the horizontal axis (importance of relationships). Figure 6.3 portrays the conflict strategies you should consider under the following conditions.

Figure 6.3
Conflict Resolution Strategies

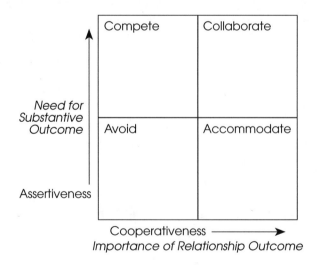

1. Use the strategy of *collaboration* when both relationship and substantive outcomes are important. Openness between you and your faculty would be the hallmark of this strategy in order to achieve a win-win outcome.

2. If you are more concerned with establishing a positive relationship with faculty over substantive goals, then strategies toward *accommodation* would be more appropriate. This is a "yield-win" strategy which allows relationships to be strengthened when outcomes may not be that important.

3. *Competing* occurs when you believe substantive interests are of more concern than relationships. Use this strategy when you have little trust in your faculty or when faculty interests are detrimental to departmental goals or outcomes. Essentially you end up with a win-lose solution because you have traded off outcome for a neutral or even poor relationship with faculty.

4. If neither substantive outcome nor relationships are important to you, *avoidance* allows you to withdraw from the issue. Rather than avoid by default, this strategy allows you to avoid confrontation when you believe the conflict may be resolved without intervention or when you need time or additional information.

These four strategies provide you with a proactive dimension to conflict responses. Presumably department chairs strive to maintain positive relationships with their faculty members and therefore should seek *resolution* while preserving the best interests of all the parties—the third and final R of conflict management.

CONFLICT RESOLUTION

The final R in creative conflict management is the search for long-term *resolution* to satisfy both parties' interests and concerns. In preparation for long-term solutions, some time for analysis is important. Answers to several questions can provide you with a framework for analyzing the conflict situation (Raiffa, 1982).

1. *Are there more than two parties?* Visualize yourself sitting across the table from another chairperson discussing the possible merger of two programs in your respective departments. The

question here is whether both of you represent all the interests and concerns which should be considered, or are other constituencies and interested parties lined up behind each of you representing your "vertical" teams (Figure 6.4A)? While both of you may agree on the terms of a merger, have you forgotten to consult your vertical teams: the faculty, staff, students, and equally important, the alumni, who represent a powerful force for tradition? Before you enter an agreement with another chair or anyone else, consider the vertical teams behind each of you and analyze what interests they might have represented in the decision.

Figure 6.4 A: The Vertical Team

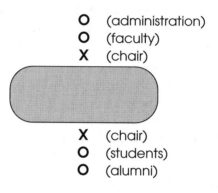

O   (administration)
O   (faculty)
X   (chair)

X   (chair)
O   (students)
O   (alumni)

---

2. *Are the parties monolithic?* Rather than an exception, it is probably the rule that both sides of a dispute are not internally monolithic. This question addresses your "horizontal" team, the person figuratively sitting next to you on your side of the table (Figure 6.4B). Are both of you monolithic in your interests? Probably not. Take the classic case of the defending attorney and client. Both want resolution to the dispute but the client's interest may be to resolve the case immediately to take care of bills, expedite time and satisfy other interests. However, the attorney, who may be paid by billable hours or a percentage of the settlement, may want to hold out for a larger portion of the settlement.

Figure 6.4 B: The Horizontal Team

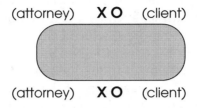

(attorney) **X O** (client)

(attorney) **X O** (client)

---

3. *Are there linkage effects?* One agreement may have an effect on another. If you agree to dispense funds for one faculty member's professional travel based on certain principles, the same principles should be used for the next request. Your decisions, therefore, should be based on sound and defensible principles.

4. *Is there more than one issue?* Confrontations with multiple issues require trade-offs and often present difficult analytical problems. If multiple issues exist, develop a hierarchy from which you can analyze each issue against another and make your trade-offs.

5. *Is ratification among faculty required?* Remember Chapter Five outlined several types of decisions available to you, from leader-centered to group-centered. For example, make sure that if conflict about the alternative solutions is likely and you have goal congruence, your decision should be taken to faculty for ratification or endorsement.

6. *Are threats possible?* While physical threats are highly unlikely, recognize that tenured faculty have a great deal of power and can make your job very uncomfortable and difficult. You need to consider the possible threats that may surface from your decisions and take the most appropriate action.

7. *Are negotiations public or private?* What you state in an open faculty meeting has significantly more impact than what you might negotiate with an individual behind closed doors. Choose your words carefully in public forums since you may "lose face" and your reputation if you are forced to reverse your decision.

8. *Is there a time constraint or time-related cost?* Clearly the closer you are to a deadline, such as a contract or the start of an academic year, the more powerful the need to resolve the issue. For example, when the North Vietnamese came to Paris to seek a settlement to the Vietnam War, they rented a house on a two-year lease and let that fact be known. The party who has to negotiate in haste is disadvantaged.

Answers to these questions can help you reach a wise and thoughtful settlement. Analysis is essential to effective conflict resolution. Exercise 6.2 allows you to use the eight basic organizing questions in analyzing one of your departmental predicaments. You will find that if you use these questions to prepare for critical conflict situations, it will be easier to be "principled" in your approach.

Exercise 6.2
Organizing Questions for Conflict Framework Development

Instructions: Recall or recreate a conflict scenario you have had in your department. Next analyze the key points according the following eight organizing questions.

1. Are there more than two parties involved in this case? If so, identify them and develop a vertical team diagram (see Figure 6.4A).

2. Are the individuals on each side of this issue monolithic in their interests? If not, outline their separate interests and develop a horizontal team diagram (see Figure 6.4B).

3. Are there linkage effects?

4. Is there more than one issue involved in this decision? If so, outline the issues and rank them to consider the proper trade-offs.

5. Is approval of the decision required by the faculty?

6. Are faculty threats possible? If so, identify them and how you might defuse them?

7. Have the negotiations been public or private? Discuss the merits and limitations of the situation.

8. Is there a time constraint involved in this case? If so, how might you deal with this condition?

PRINCIPLED CONFLICT RESOLUTION

Overall, chairs must be cautious that the *relationship outcome* between faculty and department chairs should not be indiscriminately sacrificed to the benefit of *substantive outcome*. Fisher and Ury (1983) of the Harvard Negotiation Project discovered methods to confirm and expand this assumption. They suggest any method of resolution may be fairly judged by three criteria: (1) It should produce wise agreement (outcome); (2) It should improve or at least not damage the relationship between the people involved; and (3) It should be efficient. The first and second criteria reiterate the importance of relationships and substance. The third criterion suggests the need to address expediency and effectiveness.

The most common form of resolution is achieved through a process of positioning and repositioning which may or may not take into consideration the true interests of both parties. While it does communicate the purpose of what is wanted and where one stands in relation to the other side, positioning fails to meet the three criteria of a wise outcome. In fact, arguing over positions produces unwise agreements, is inefficient, and endangers ongoing relationships. It is critical to understand that a wise outcome is one which "meets the legitimate interests of each side to the extent possible, resolves conflicting interests fairly, is durable, and takes community interests into account" (Fisher and Ury, 1983, p.4).

The technique of principled resolution as espoused by Fisher and Ury provides a straightforward method of conflict resolution appropriate for use in almost any circumstance, especially in academic settings where both outcome and relationships are very important to achieve and maintain. If you explore the interests rather than positions of your faculty, you will build the foundation for principled conflict resolution.

Focus On Interests, Not Positions

Focusing on positions will produce win, lose, or yield results, all of which do not guarantee that both parties have achieved a satisfying, long-term resolution. As outlined in Table 6.3, interests are the basic intangible or abstract needs of a party such as values, principles, or psychological or physiological needs. Needs are rarely talked about when parties come into conflict situations, and are also very difficult to clarify because they are not often negotiable, usually intangible, and not measurable. Some of the needs expressed by faculty are such things as security, economic well-being, social acceptance, power, recognition, control and autonomy. A negotiable and measurable position is tenure, promotion or salary, but the personal interests of security, equity, recognition and power are probably at the root of most faculty-chair conflicts. The bottom line is that interest satisfaction must be achieved if conflict is to be resolved.

Table 6.3
Exploring Faculty Interests

Definition

> The basic intangible or abstract needs of faculty such as values, principles, or needs

Characteristics

> Rarely negotiable
> Usually intangible
> Not measurable

Results

> Interest satisfaction must be achieved if reform is to be accepted

---

Reflect for a moment, refer back to the situation in Exercise 6.2, and see if you can identify what faculty interests were imbedded in the conflict situation you chose. Are you having difficulty? Use Exercise 6.3 to guide your thinking. Remember that their needs may be as basic as security, such as tenure, or equity in the form of pay and rewards.

Exercise 6.3
Faculty Interest Inventory

Instructions: The foundation of conflict resolution is built on the knowledge that you can articulate the interests of your faculty. On the matrix below, identify your faculty members down the right side of the page and across the top write your perception of each faculty member's primary interest and secondary interest.

Remember, interests are intangible or abstract needs of individuals such as values, principles or motivations. They are rarely negotiable, usually intangible, and not measurable.

Faculty Member	Primary Interest	Secondary Interest
A.		
B.		
C.		
D.		
E.		
F.		
G.		

While interests create the foundation for principled resolution, three other practices provide the mortar to secure the foundation.

1. *People: Separate people from the problem.* In the days of demonstrations and civil disobedience in the 1950s and 1960s the book by Saul Alinsky, *Rules for Radicals* (1971) taught the opposite: attack the person psychologically and once the ego gets involved, you have the advantage. Principled resolution avoids personal attacks and does not impute personal feelings or concerns to others. Recognize the individual and try to identify your faculty's interests by actively listening and empathizing with their needs. If you become committed to a particular idea or position, your ego can get connected to your

position. Your energies may then be directed toward your own defense and you may attack rather than trying to solve the problem. In contrast, focusing on the problem allows the interests and perceptions of both parties to be explored without personal attacks which can destroy relationships.

2. *Options: Generate a variety of possibilities before deciding what to do.* Avoid premature judgments or locking in on positions before assumptions are examined and interests are explored. Once you and your faculty lock into your respective positions, your discussions will include only those options between position A and position B. Therefore, a compromise solution somewhere between A and B remains as the only resolution. One or both of you will lose at least partially.

In fact, a solution (point C) may exist, not even on the A-B line, which creatively satisfies the needs of both parties. For example, if you have a limited amount of salary money available to disperse among faculty members, rather than arguing with a faculty member between your position of $3,000 and his/her position of $4,000, maybe the faculty member may settle for an extra $500 to $1,000 travel expense allocation out of a more plentiful source of funds (point C).

3. *Criteria: Base resolution on objective standards.* Department chairs and faculty must find fair standards and procedures to achieve the desired end results. Bring standards of fairness, efficiency, or merit into the discussion and you will be more likely to produce a wise and fair resolution. In position resolution, you will spend time and energy defending your position and attacking the other side. If you base your agreement on consistent standards such as precedent, equal treatment, tradition, market value, moral codes or professional ethics you will be less vulnerable to attack. In this search for resolution both you and your faculty must yield to principle, not to pressure, and keep the focus on interests.

To summarize, the principled method, in contrast to positional resolution, focuses on basic interests of both you and your faculty, while searching for mutually satisfying options based on fair standards and procedures which typically will lead to wise outcomes or agreements (see Table 6.4). Once you separate personalities from the problems, you will be able to deal with faculty empathetically as human beings in search for a satisfying resolution and amicable agreement.

Traditionally, the positional resolution of conflict has taken sides, either through hard or soft negotiations. Chairs, in turn are often typed as one side of the Janus face or the other, either faculty or administration—either for faculty interests or against them in favor of administrative needs. The soft department chair emphasizes the importance of building and maintaining relationships so that they approach conflict as friends, seeking agreement, making offers, and yielding to pressure. In contrast, the hard department chair sees faculty as adversaries who seek victory, make threats and apply pressures.

Table 6.4
Principled Conflict Resolution Skills

I. Don't bargain over position since it often:
   - endangers ongoing relationships.
   - becomes difficult when more than two parties are involved.
   - places all parties in a win/lose situation.

II. Separate the people from the problem
   - recognize the individual
   - look for perceptions (actively listen, empathize)
   - don't impute your feelings or concerns to others
   - avoid personal attacks

III. Focus on interests
   - behind each position lies both differing and compatible interests
   - identify interests (explore the why's and why not's)
   - look forward—not back
   - be hard on the problem, be soft on the people

IV. Invent options
   - avoid premature judgments, examine your assumptions
   - be creative
   - look for mutual benefit (not win/lose)
   - find additional resources, remove obstacles

V. Use objective criteria
   - find fair standards, fair procedures
   - establish common purpose, desired end results
   - yield to principle—not to pressure

Source: Fisher, R. & Ury, W. (1983). *Getting to Yes.*

However, you do not have to choose between hard or soft styles of resolution. The above principles empower you to change the rules of the game and approach conflict from a principled point of view so you can work with faculty as mutual problem solvers, seeking wise outcomes by exploring interests and yielding to principle, not pressure. Table 6.5 displays the contrasting highlights of these three conflict resolution approaches.

Table 6.5
Ways to Resolve Conflict

Soft	Hard	Principled
Friends	Adversaries	Problem Solver
Agreement	Victory	Wise Outcome
Trust	Distrust	Independent of Trust
Make Offers	Make Threats	Explore Interests
Yield to Pressure	Apply Pressure	Yield to Principle, Not Pressure

THE DEPARTMENT CHAIR AS MEDIATOR

The preceding discussion on resolution may lead you to believe that your primary role in conflict is to negotiate an equitable settlement, protecting the interests of others and yourself at the same time. This assumes that you, personally, are in conflict with someone else: a student, faculty member, dean, or even another chair. However, you should recognize your important role in assisting with the resolution of conflict among these other groups as well. In addition to developing negotiation skills, you should also understand the roles and skills required to mediate other people's conflict.

While the role of negotiator is often intuitively understood, mediation requires a different process and set of skills. Chairs as mediators need to perform the roles of conflict assessor, process convener, resource expander, reality tester, and active listener.

The mediation process itself follows a different resolution pattern than the traditional negotiation session. As developed by several dispute resolution centers in the Western world, mediation follows a distinct procedure (Lincoln & O'Donnell, 1986;

Moses & Roe, 1990). It is as much a science as an art. If you, as chair, accept the role of mediator, eight generic procedures should be used in the mediation process.

1. *Clarify the chair's role as mediator.* The mediator's main role is to get both sides to suggest solutions and not to make the final decision. Therefore, your role is to be impartial and facilitate the presentation of facts, feelings and proposals. In order to do this, you must remain objective and represent both sides of the disagreement, use supportive and nonjudgmental language, and create a nonthreatening environment where the disputants feel comfortable and safe in expressing themselves, their needs and their aspirations. You must also help the parties understanding of each other's needs and interests and facilitate a mutually acceptable solution.

2. *Invite opening statements from the disputants.* Have each of the disputants separately make opening statements as to their expectations of the mediation process. Reinforce that mediation is a voluntary process that can be terminated at any time.

3. *Develop presentation of issues and feelings.* As in a court of law, have the charging party go first and lay out the facts and feelings of their side of the case. The other side then shares their side of the story. Your responsibility is to actively listen and have the parties generate data.

4. *Clarify and elaborate the facts.* At this point you may ask for clarification of perceptions and verification of the facts as stated by each party. You may need to ask for more detail on specific issues and even have the parties repeat what was said as a means of sorting out errors in understanding. Through the use of summarization and paraphrasing, ensure appreciation and understanding of each other's point of view.

5. *Help the parties move toward resolution.* Assess whether both parties are willing to begin resolving the conflict. In full session or by private caucus, ask for proposed remedies or points on which they agree, then help them isolate the issues which need to be resolved. You should realize that mediation may extend over a period of several sessions, with caucusing and perception-checking taking place in-between sessions.

6. *Solicit suggestions and contributions.* Have each of the parties equally contribute to solutions which may satisfy both of their needs. The more they develop their own solution, the more likely they will be to feel committed to uphold it.

7. *Reality-test solutions.* Once they have proposed solutions, ask how they arrive at them. Based on what criteria? How would the suggested solution satisfy the other party's interests? Remember, interest satisfaction must be achieved if conflict is to be resolved.

8. *Summarize agreement and commitment.* It is your role to summarize what has been agreed and commit them to it, either in writing or by your witness as an objective third party. Each must leave with a clear picture of what has been achieved and what each party is obligated to do. While some conflicts may not be totally resolved, they may be better managed in the future.

Finally, congratulate both parties and reinforce anything they have found useful in resolving the current dispute. Remember, it is critical for the mediator to be objective, neutral, and non-aligned with either party (Moses & Roe, 1990). However, this neutral role poses some problems if the parties have disproportionate power bases and abilities to articulate their cases. You must then assume a role in encouraging the less vocal faculty to speak up and express needs, for the minority opinions today may be the majority tomorrow.

INGREDIENTS FOR SATISFYING RESOLUTION

Regardless of the approach you use to resolve conflict in your department, whether it be mediation or negotiation, the key is in its durability and how it will stand up over time. This long-term solution comes from each party's sense of satisfaction in three areas: procedural satisfaction, substantive satisfaction and psychological satisfaction (Lincoln & O'Donnell, 1986). If either of the parties have a high degree of dissatisfaction in any of these three areas, there is great likelihood that the agreement may be short lived and result in conflict aftermath. In order to avoid conflict aftermath you must make sure that each party obtains all three levels of satisfaction.

Procedural Satisfaction

The basic question is whether the parties were satisfied with the conflict proceedings before, during and after the resolution. Who initiated the process? Where did the meetings take place? Were the meetings in your office, a faculty member's office, or in a neutral place such as a conference room or the student union cafeteria? The parties must feel they had control over the process and were not forced into any unusual or uncomfortable, or disadvantageous procedures. The ultimate test of procedural satisfaction is whether the parties would use the same process again.

Substantive Satisfaction

While conflict response styles speak to trading-off substance against relationships, it is imperative that no matter what the trade-off, both parties must feel a sense of adequate resolution. This can only be present if a reasonable level of interest satisfaction is achieved. The key to substantive satisfaction is not ultimate resolution for one party over another, but an acceptable level of satisfaction for both.

Psychological Satisfaction

As is the case with substantive satisfaction, a balance between relationships and substance must be achieved if parties are to be psychologically satisfied. If both parties feel better after resolution than before, psychological satisfaction has most likely occurred. Rather than feeling like a winner or loser, each disputant should have a sense of equity in the resolution and ownership in the solution.

CONCLUSION

In conclusion, there is probably very little in this chapter which you do not already know, intuitively. The purpose is to expose you to the issues surrounding conflict management and help you organize your conflict resolution approach into a creative, useable framework of the three R's of conflict: *recognition*, *response* and *resolution*.

This is not a chapter on how to win in battle against faculty, but how to deal with interests such that you and your faculty find satisfying resolution while enjoying mutual respect and maintaining positive and productive relationships. If you believe the principles discussed in this chapter will help you, share them with your adversaries. Unlike most other strategies, if the other side becomes equally skilled, it becomes easier, not more difficult to reach agreement. The next step is yours. As a wise old Chinese philosopher once said: "To know, and not to use, is not yet to know." Use it so you may now know it.

7

COPING WITH STRESS: MAINTAINING YOUR ENTHUSIASM

*T**he morning begins with the sound of the alarm, a hurried break-
fast, a quick kiss to spouse and kids, to the harried push-and-shove
to get one of the limited parking spaces, and to the office just prior to the
arrival of faculty and staff. If the chair is lucky, the early arrival permits
a cursory perusal of the day's tasks, commitments and committee meetings. Planning time is abruptly interrupted by the onslaught of urgent
calls, crises, and calendar changes. Five cups of coffee, four faculty drop-
ins, three committee meetings, two irate students, and one call from a
demanding dean later, the chair realizes that it's time to find some fast
food at the student union on the way to the next appointment.*

*The early afternoon is productive but hectic, saved by a blocked
period of time for planning and returning telephone calls. But alas, an
urgent faculty problem has co-opted the chair's late afternoon schedule.*

*In the evening, family commitments come second to the endless
alumni meetings, clubs, and social events that a chair is expected to attend.
Monday through Friday is spent reacting to the urgent demands of faculty, students and the higher levels of administration, while Saturdays,
Sundays, and evenings seem to be the only times a chair can keep up with
the paperwork and ponder future plans in a more proactive manner.*

INTRODUCTION

Chairs love to help students and colleagues, that is why they
are chairs, but the stress headache and activated peptic ulcer at
the end of a frenzied day forces many department chairs to

return to faculty status after serving a single term. What is known about this phenomenon called stress? And what can academics do to control stress and make the job of department chair more satisfying?

This chapter focuses on strategies for coping with stress. First, you will explore the nature of stress and dispel the common myths which cloud the issues of stress control. Next, the chair stress cycle introduces you to a four-stage model which provides a framework for managing your stress. Finally, you will explore each stage of the stress cycle and identify techniques to master the stresses of chairing a department. In addition, your role as stress filter for your faculty and staff will be examined with suggestions for assisting your colleagues in coping with their stress traps.

COMMON MYTHS ABOUT STRESS

To help clarify some of the misconceptions surrounding the concept of stress over the past few decades, focus your attention on the following myths.

Myth #1: *Stress is harmful.* While the popular connotation portrays an image that stress is unpleasant or negative, it can be positive as well. The Chinese, for example, represent stress with two characters, one signalling danger and the other opportunity. Like the Chinese representation, stress today actually encompasses both distress (bad or unpleasant events) and eustress (good or pleasant events). Through slurring, the old French and Middle English word distress came into common English usage as stress, with its sole negative connotation in the Western world. Failure is stressful, but so is success.

Myth #2: *Stress should be avoided.* Stress is a natural part of life and helps individuals respond to threat or rise to challenge. In essence, it cannot and should not be avoided, for without stress you could not live. What "under stress" actually means is that you are under "excessive" stress or distress. An analogous condition is that of "running a temperature," meaning above normal. Body temperature itself is essential to life, just as is stress. Stress cannot be avoided, other than by death. Therefore, chairs should not always seek to avoid stress; it can be the spice of life, when handled properly.

Myth #3: *The higher up in the organization the greater the stress.* It is popularly believed that high-level executives lead the list of heart disease patients. However, a Metropolitan Life Insurance Company study challenged this assumption when it found that presidents and vice-presidents of the 500 largest industrial corporations suffered 40% fewer heart attack deaths than middle managers of the same companies. Similar data support the conclusion that middle managers have a higher peptic ulcer rate than chief executive officers. Results in academe are mixed on who suffers the most from stress; one study found that department chairs reported greater stress than all other classifications of faculty (resident instructional faculty, librarians, student services, and cooperative extension) as well as other academic administrators (Gmelch and Wilke, 1991). In a comparative study of 23 occupations, professors in administrative posts ranked first , ahead of professors (ranked sixth), in reported stresses and strains (Caplan, et al., 1980). In addition, faculty professors reported more satisfaction with their jobs than professors serving as administrators.

Myth #4: *Stress is a male-dominated phenomena.* Until the 1980s, the literature commonly referred to "men under stress." While this male pronoun myth or misguided reference no longer prevails, it is a well-known fact that men suffer higher rates of alcoholism, ulcers, lung cancer, suicide and heart disease than women. However, as the number of women in male-dominated professions increases, so do the incidences of stress and stress-related diseases. In a national study of professorial stress, women reported more stress than men, and married women experienced even more stress than single women professors (Gmelch, Lovrich and Wilke, 1984).

Myth #5: *There is one right way to cope with stress.* Researchers have addressed popular and academic concerns as well as conceptual, theoretical, and empirical investigations on coping and the answer to effective coping processes remains elusive. With the recent interest in educator stress, it is surprising to find little attention given to the precise ways educators cope with stress.

THE CHAIR STRESS CYCLE

As a department chair, rather than avoiding stress, you need to control it and use it to your advantage. The four-stage Chair

Stress Cycle portrayed in Figure 7.1 provides a broad perspective and clear understanding of stress, and introduces a framework for action. The process begins with Stage I, *stressors*, a set of specific demands. Excessive meetings, interruptions, and confrontations represent some common chair stressors. How much stress is produced by these stressors depends on Stage II, the department chair's *perception* of these demands. If you do not have the physical or mental resources to meet the demand, you perceive the demand as a stress trap. Stress created by this discrepancy between *demand* and *personal resources* results in a specific stress *response*—Stage III. The fourth and final stage, *consequences*, pertains to the intensity and long-range negative effects of stress.

Figure 7.1
The Chair Stress Cycle

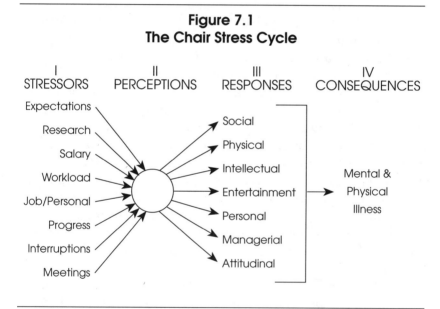

The stress cycle defines stress as: *One's anticipation of his or her inability to respond (Stage III) adequately to perceived (Stage II) demands (Stage I), accompanied by the anticipation of negative consequences (Stage IV) due to inadequate responses.* Note the negative connotation of this definition—distress or negative stress resulting from harm or threats. However, your stress can be positive, resulting from challenge or excitement. Therefore you can transform this negative definition into a positive response by changing your perception from *inability* to ability: The anticipation of your *ability* to respond adequately to a perceived demand, accompanied by your anticipation of a *positive* consequence for an *adequate* response.

This chapter focuses on all four stages of the stress cycle: identify stressors in Stage I; investigate your proneness to stressful personality types in Stage II; broaden your repertoire of effective coping responses in Stage III; and convert the possible negative consequences in Stage IV from illness to wellness through a stress absorbers plan. If the stressors can be identified, negative perceptions turned into positive ones, and a variety of responses utilized in numerous ways, then the consequence will be a healthy and productive department chair.

DEPARTMENT CHAIR STRESS TRAPS: STAGE I

You can begin to control your four-stage stress cycle by examining the demands of your current situation. What are your stress traps as department chair? Meetings, interruptions, staff conflicts, drop-in visitors, and rules and regulations all represent potential stressors. While a single telephone interruption may not cause a great deal of difficulty, couple the interruption with unexpected and unwanted drop-in visitors, irate faculty members, or a backlog of paperwork, and you're likely to find some prime, personal stress traps. The key to stress reduction rests with identifying your stress traps. It may help to understand the more common stressors of department chairs.

Table 7.1 includes 41 common causes of department chair stress developed from a series of national and institutional studies. In order to ensure that all potentially relevant facets of chair-related stress were identified, the items on the Chair Stress Inventory (CSI) were compiled from several sources. First, chairs kept stress logs for a period of two weeks in order to indicate on a daily basis the most stressful single event and the most stressful series of events. Next a survey was conducted of chair job descriptions in search of additional stressors not already discovered by the stress logs. Third, other instruments developed to assess stress in academe were investigated for additional items. Finally, two studies of department chairs were conducted, one at a comprehensive university (Gmelch & Wilke, 1991) and another of department chairs in 100 institutions of higher education (Gmelch & Burns, 1991). The compilation of items from all four sources resulted in the 41-item Chair Stress Inventory.

Table 7.1
Ranking of Stressors

Rank	Stress Questionnaire Item	Mean
1.	Having insufficient time to stay current in my academic field	3.9
2.	Trying to gain financial support for department programs	3.5
3.	Evaluating faculty and staff performance	3.4
4.	Attending meetings which take up too much time	3.3
5.	Feeling I have too heavy a workload	3.3
6.	Believing my academic career progress is not what it should be	3.3
7.	Writing letters and memos, and responding to other paperwork	3.2
8.	Imposing excessively high self-expectations	3.2
9.	Preparing manuscripts for publication	3.1
10.	Meeting report and other paperwork deadlines	3.1
11.	Making decisions that affect the lives of faculty, staff and students	3.1
12.	Preparing budgets and allocating resources	3.0
13.	Seeking compatibility among institutional, departmental and personal goals	3.0
14.	Securing financial support for my research	2.9
15.	Feeling required paperwork is not utilized	2.9
16.	Having inadequate time for teaching preparation	2.9
17.	Complying with college and university rules and regulations	2.8
18.	Participating in work-related activities outside regular hours	2.8
19.	Trying to influence the actions and decisions of my dean	2.7
20.	Receiving insufficient recognition for performing administrative responsibilities	2.7
21.	Handling student concerns and conflicts	2.7
22.	Supervising and coordinating the tasks of many people	2.6
23.	Receiving inadequate salary	2.6
24.	Having insufficient authority to perform my departmental responsibilities	2.4
25.	Resolving differences with my dean	2.3

Rank	Stress Questionnaire Item	Mean
26.	Trying to satisfy the concerns of constituent groups (alumni, community, etc.)	2.2
27.	Meeting social obligations (clubs, parties, volunteer work) expected of chairs	2.2
28.	Feeling others don't understand my goals and expectations	2.1
29.	Having a non-conducive work environment (e.g. crowded, noisy, inadequate facilities)	2.1
30.	Not knowing how my dean evaluates my performance	2.1
31.	Receiving insufficient recognition for research performance	2.1
32.	Feeling I will not be able to satisfy the conflicting demands of those in positions of authority over me	2.0
33.	Believing I can't get all of the information I need to carry out my job properly	2.0
34.	Making presentations at professional meetings	1.9
35.	Adapting to technological changes (e.g. fax, telephone systems, computers)	1.8
36.	Having to travel to fulfill job expectations	1.8
37.	Feeling I am not adequately trained to handle my job	1.7
38.	Believing my administrative career progress is not what it should be	1.7
39.	Feeling pressure for better job performance above what I feel is reasonable	1.6
40.	Feeling I have too much responsibility delegated to me by my dean	1.6
41.	Feeling not enough is expected of me by my dean	1.3

Note: Stress scale ranges from 5 (most stressful) to 1 (least stressful).

Source: Burns, J.S. and Gmelch, W.H. (1992). Center for the Study of the Department Chair, Washington State University.

Factors of Department Chair Stress

Rather than assessing the impact of individual stressors, another method of reviewing and analyzing your stressors is to find themes of department chair stress. A factor analysis of the chair stressors discloses five themes, displayed in Table 7.2: administrative tasks, faculty role, role ambiguity, hierarchical authority, and perceived expectations (Burns, 1992).

TABLE 7.2
Factors of Department Chair Stress

1. Administrative Task Stress

Meeting report and other paperwork deadlines

Preparing budgets and allocating resources

Trying to gain financial support for department programs

Writing letters, memos, and responding to other paperwork

Evaluating faculty and staff performance

Having to make decisions that affect the lives of faculty, staff
and students

Feeling I have too heavy a workload

Supervising and coordinating the tasks of many people

Complying with college and university rules and regulations

Attending meetings which take up too much time

Handling student concerns and conflicts

Seeking compatibility among institutional, departmental
and personal goals

2. Faculty Role Stress

Preparing manuscripts for publication

Securing financial support for my research

Believing my academic career progress is not what it should be

Receiving insufficient recognition for research performance

Having insufficient time to stay current in my academic field

3. Role Ambiguity Stress

Feeling I am not adequately trained to handle my job

Feeling I have too much responsibility delegated to me by
my dean

Feeling not enough is expected of me by my dean

Believing I can't get all the information I need to carry out my job

Feeling others don't understand my goals and expectations

Trying to satisfy the concerns of constituent groups (alumni,
community...)

4. Hierarchical Authority Stress

Not knowing how my dean evaluates my performance

Trying to influence the actions and decisions of my dean

Receiving insufficient recognition for administrative
responsibilities

Having insufficient authority to perform my departmental
responsibilities

Feeling I will not be able to satisfy the conflicting demands
with those in positions of authority over me

Resolving differences with my dean

Feeling pressure for better job performance above what I feel
is reasonable

Believing my administrative career progress is not what is
should be

Feeling required paperwork is not utilized

Receiving inadequate salary

5. Perceived Expectations Stress

Having to travel to fulfill job expectations

Participating in work-related activities outside regular working
hours which conflict with personal activities

Meeting social obligations (clubs, parties, volunteer work)
expected of chairs

Making presentations at professional meetings

Imposing excessively high self-expectations

Source: Center for the Study of the Department Chair, Washington State University,
1992.

Administrative tasks deals with three areas of managerial roles
and responsibilities: administrative details in terms of meetings,
workload, paperwork, deadlines, and budgets and financial support; personnel administration including handling student conflicts, evaluating staff and faculty, supervising and coordinating
personnel, and having to make decisions that affect the lives of
faculty, staff and students; and organizational constraints highlighting the frustrations of complying with college and university
regulations and seeking compatibility among institutional,
departmental and individual goals.

Secondly, department chairs seem to be caught between the
previous common administrative stresses and those of the regular
faculty role: keeping current in their discipline, preparing manuscripts, searching for money for their research, and making presentations. In addition, they feel that their academic career
progress is not what it should be, possibly due to serving as
department chair. Thus, chairs are trapped between the pressures
and demands of performing not only as an administrator, but also
as a productive faculty member.

From this Janus position emerges the *role ambiguity* factor. As indicated in Table 7.2, chairs basically experience stress from the uncertainties, inadequacies, and performance cues of the chair position. These uncertainties reflect the typical research descriptions of role ambiguity (Kahn et al., 1964). This recurring "academic administrator" Janus theme (chair as faculty—chair as administrator) emerges again when comparing the most serious stressors of chairs with those of faculty. Table 7.3 contrasts two national stress studies, one of chairs (Gmelch & Burns, 1990) and the other of college faculty (Gmelch, Wilke & Lovrich, 1984). Note first that not only do chairs identify seven of the professors' most serious stressors as their own, but the percent of chairs suffering from these stressors is higher in each case except for "excessively high self-expectations" (typically more troublesome for faculty than administrative positions). This paradoxical situation of trying to fill a "swivel" position causes department chairs to feel double pressure to be an effective manager and productive faculty member.

Chairs' responsibility as a representative of the department to the dean and higher administration is encompassed in the *hierarchical authority* stress factor. This theme contains six stressors involving relationships with the dean and higher authorities. Additional frustrations from this area include the elements of inadequate recognition, rewards and career progression.

Finally, and probably most problematic for department chairs, is the fifth factor, *perceived expectations*, which reflects the commitments and obligations chairs perceive as necessary to fulfill the expectations of their positions, such as travel, social commitments and volunteer work. The most notable and powerful stressor in this factor is self-imposed "excessively high self-expectations." In other words, it may not be the influence of an oppressive hierarchy or demanding dean that causes the greatest concern as much as the stress within one's self from expecting more than can be delivered.

To what extent do each of these chair stress traps cause you concern? Some will bother you more than others. Read through each item of the Chair Stress Inventory in Exercise 7.1 and rate them from "1" (rarely or never stressful) to "5" (frequently stressful). Identify your ten most bothersome chair stressors. In addition, calculate which factor of chair stress causes you the greatest concern. As a reference point, from a national study of 800 department chairs, Table 7.4 reveals the 10 most serious stressors faced by department chairs, in addition to the ranking of chair stress factors.

Table 7.3
Comparison of Chair and Professor Stress

Stressors	Chairs		Professors	
	Rank	Serious Stress	Rank	Serious Stress
Heavy workload	1	59%	5.5	40%
Obtaining program approval	2	54%	N/A	N/A
Keeping current	3	53%	3	49%
Complying with rules	4	48%	-	-
Job interfering/personal time	5	47%	7	35%
Decisions affecting others	6	46%	-	-
Excessive self-expectations	7	45%	1	53%
Resolving collegial differences	8	45%	-	-
Evaluating faculty	9	42%	N/A	N/A
Completing paperwork	10	41%	-	-
Preparing manuscripts	11	40%	5.5	40%
Telephone/visitor interruptions	12	40%	9.5	33%
Meetings	13	40%	9.5	33%

Source: Gmelch, W.H. and Burns, J.S. (1993). A National Study of Stress and Department Chairs. *Innovative Higher Education.*

Exercise 7.1
Chair Stress Inventory

The following work-related situations have been identified as potential sources of stress. It is likely that some of these situations cause you more concern than others. Indicate to what extent each is a source of work-related stress by checking the appropriate response.

	Level of Stress:	Slight 1	2	Moderate 3	4	High 5
1.	Participating in work-related activities outside regular working hours which conflict with personal time	☐	☐	☐	☐	☐
2.	Meeting social obligations (clubs, parties, volunteer work) expected of chairs	☐	☐	☐	☐	☐
3.	Complying with college and university rules and regulations	☐	☐	☐	☐	☐
4.	Having a non-conducive work environment (e.g. crowded, noisy, inadequate facilities)	☐	☐	☐	☐	☐
5.	Making presentations at professional meetings	☐	☐	☐	☐	☐
6.	Imposing excessively high self-expectations	☐	☐	☐	☐	☐
7.	Handling student concerns and conflicts	☐	☐	☐	☐	☐
8.	Resolving differences with my dean/supervisor	☐	☐	☐	☐	☐
9.	Having insufficient time to stay current in my academic field	☐	☐	☐	☐	☐
10.	Having insufficient authority to perform my departmental responsibilities	☐	☐	☐	☐	☐
11.	Believing my administrative career progress is not what it should be	☐	☐	☐	☐	☐
12.	Believing my academic career progress is not what it should be	☐	☐	☐	☐	☐
13.	Having to travel to fulfill job expectations	☐	☐	☐	☐	☐
14.	Securing financial support for my research	☐	☐	☐	☐	☐
15.	Preparing manuscripts for publication	☐	☐	☐	☐	☐
16.	Receiving insufficient recognition for performing administrative responsibilities	☐	☐	☐	☐	☐
17.	Feeling required paperwork is not utilized	☐	☐	☐	☐	☐
18.	Having inadequate time for teaching preparation	☐	☐	☐	☐	☐
19.	Writing letters and memos, and responding to other paperwork	☐	☐	☐	☐	☐
20.	Feeling I have too heavy a workload	☐	☐	☐	☐	☐
21.	Attending meetings which take up too much time	☐	☐	☐	☐	☐
22.	Trying to influence the actions and decisions of my dean/supervisor	☐	☐	☐	☐	☐
23.	Adapting to technological changes (e.g., fax, telephone systems, computers)	☐	☐	☐	☐	☐

	Level of Stress:	**Slight**		**Moderate**		**High**
		1	**2**	**3**	**4**	**5**
24.	Seeking compatibility among institutional, departmental, and personal goals	☐	☐	☐	☐	☐
25.	Receiving insufficient recognition for research performance	☐	☐	☐	☐	☐
26.	Not knowing how my dean/supervisor evaluates my performance	☐	☐	☐	☐	☐
27.	Receiving inadequate salary	☐	☐	☐	☐	☐
28.	Evaluating faculty and staff performance	☐	☐	☐	☐	☐
29.	Trying to satisfy the concerns of constituent groups (alumni, community, etc.)	☐	☐	☐	☐	☐
30.	Supervising and coordinating the tasks of many people	☐	☐	☐	☐	☐
31.	Feeling others don't understand my goals and expectations	☐	☐	☐	☐	☐
32.	Feeling I am not adequately trained to handle my job	☐	☐	☐	☐	☐
33.	Believing I can't get all of the information I need to carry out my job properly	☐	☐	☐	☐	☐
34.	Feeling I will not be able to satisfy the conflicting demands of those in positions of authority over me	☐	☐	☐	☐	☐
35.	Feeling not enough is expected of me by my dean/supervisor	☐	☐	☐	☐	☐
36.	Feeling pressure for better job performance above what I feel is reasonable	☐	☐	☐	☐	☐
37.	Having to make decisions that affect the lives of faculty, staff, and students	☐	☐	☐	☐	☐
38.	Feeling I have too much responsibility delegated to me by my dean/supervisor	☐	☐	☐	☐	☐
39.	Meeting report and other paperwork deadlines	☐	☐	☐	☐	☐
40.	Preparing budgets and allocating resources	☐	☐	☐	☐	☐
41.	Trying to gain financial support for departmental programs	☐	☐	☐	☐	☐

Assess the overall level of stress you experience as a chair   ☐ ☐ ☐ ☐ ☐

What percentage of the total stress in your life results from being a department chair?   _____%

Table 7.4
Top Department Chair Stressors

I. Insufficient time to keep current in academic field

2. Gaining financial support for department programs

3. Evaluating faculty and staff performance

4. Attending meetings which take up too much time

5. Feeling I have too heavy a workload

6. Believing my academic career progress is not what it should be

7. Writing letters, memos, and responding to other paperwork

8. Imposing excessively high self-expectations

9. Preparing manuscripts for publication

10. Meeting report and other paperwork deadlines

Source: Center for the Study of the Department Chair, Washington State University, 1992.

THE PERCEPTION OF STRESS: STAGE II

While demands surrounding the chair position cannot always be diminished, our perception, attitude and approach is under our control and is, after all, the deciding factor in whether these demands become stress traps. Nervous, tense and uptight feelings are usually attributed to outside conditions rather than looking within ourselves. Professors and chairs alike typically blame the upper-level college or university administration, state or corporate funding, regents or other demanding clientele for placing pressures to perform beyond one's capabilities. In actuality much of the stress experienced by academics is self-imposed. In fact, individual personalities play an important role in determining how stressful academic conditions are. Stressors, by themselves, represent objective demands which only become stress traps when one subjectively perceives them to be troublesome. Perceptions (Stage II) then become the key to whether stress is received or denied. Consider the definition of stress proposed earlier and realize the role of perception in this process.

"The anticipation (which could be real or imaginary) of your inability (the degree to which you feel prepared to perform the role of department chair) to respond adequately to a *perceived demand* (the critical element of whether stress exists or not), accompanied by your anticipation (again anticipation could be real or imaginary) of negative consequences for an inadequate response." This definition is based on your perception of your ability to meet the challenges of chairing a department. Thus, it is how you approach your job and your life that causes most of your stress. Perception plays the major role in your resilience to, or acceptance of, stress in your job. Although it is difficult to establish clear causal links between personality factors and disease, sufficient research evidence exists to document the link between certain types of behaviors and heart disease, cancer, arthritis, asthma, migraine headaches, and the like. This evidence is too strong to dismiss and too critical to overlook.

Type A Department Chairs

Of particular importance and deserving of your attention is the "coronary heart disease" personality, or Type A behavior (Friedman and Rosenman, 1974). Since heart disease remains the number one killer in the United States, managing your "Type A behavior" through perceptual awareness may save a life, even your own.

Type A's approach their jobs with intensity and impatience. So much so that they are attacked by heart disease at triple the rate of more relaxed and easygoing Type B's. But what exactly is Type A behavior and to what extent do department chairs exhibit it? A Type A chair can be characterized as an overly competitive achiever, aggressive, fast worker, impatient, restless, hyperalert, explosive in speech, tense, always feeling under pressure, insecure and unaware of his/her own limitations. In contrast, Type B behavior is the mirror opposite: relaxed, easygoing, seldom impatient, takes more time to enjoy things in life besides work, not easily irritated, works steadily, seldom lacks time, not preoccupied with social achievement, and moves and speaks more slowly.

But who are the Type A's? Are chairs more prone than faculty members? Are you Type A? A major study entitled *Job Demands and Worker Health* investigated the extent of Type A personality characteristics in 23 occupations, including professors and academic administrators (Caplan, et al., 1980). First the bad news: two occupations had by far the highest scores on the Type A index, academic administrators and family physicians. Table 7.5 shows that academic administrators (e.g. department chairs and directors) ranked first in Type A behavior (Column 1), and professors, ranked sixth. Note that the professors' scores were one-third lower on the index than academic administrators. In addition, 12 percent of the academic administrators in this study suffered from coronary heart disease (Column 2), a three times greater heart disease rate than professors (4%).

What might be some of the contributors to this higher incidence of heart disease and Type A behavior? Could it be the overtime administrators put into their jobs? Not at first glance. The third column of Table 7.5 shows that professors and academic administrators report working 12 and 16 hours, respectively, beyond the traditional forty hour week (Column 4). Nevertheless, professors report only 31 percent (3.6 hours) of their 12 hours as overtime they didn't want to work whereas academic administrators report 70 percent (11.4 hours) of their overtime hours as unwanted. In other words, the extra hours beyond the forty hour work week are seen in a more positive light by professors and in a less positive light by administrators. As a study of university professors points out, many professors consider the hours beyond a forty hour week as not overtime but simply as part of the time they need to perform their duties as they desire (French and Caplan, 1973). "I would work the hours anyway even if no one asked me," commented one professor summing up this viewpoint. The administrative professor, however, views those extra hours as busy work (Caplan et al., 1980, p. 124). All in all, academic administrators put in more unwanted overtime than any other occupation (professors are about average).

Table 7.5
Influences on Occupational Stress

Occupation	(1) Type A	(2) % Coronary Heart Disease	(3) Hours Worked per Week	(4) Overtime per Week
Administrative Professor	155	12.0	56.4	11.4
Physician	149	12.5	58.4	6.7
Tool & Die Worker	123	14.3	46.9	4.3
Administrator	111	8.3	48.7	6.4
Supervisor Blue Collar	108	4.8	47.6	6.8
Scientist	106	5.1	46.6	5.0
Professor	106	4.1	51.6	3.6
Air Traffic Controller	102	3.7	38.1	0.4
Train Dispatcher	98	9.3	41.7	2.8
Supervisor White Collar	5	4.8	43.7	3.8
Air Traffic Controller (small airport)	94	0.0	38.7	0.9
Electronic Technician	93	9.7	40.2	2.2
Police Officer	89	2.7	46.1	6.4
Forklift Driver	87	10.9	40.4	3.5
Courier	85	5.0	39.1	1.7
Assembly Worker (nonpaced)	84	5.8	41.9	5.7
Engineer	82	5.5	43.3	3.6
Machine Tender	81	5.9	42.9	4.3
Accountant	74	12.0	40.6	1.9
Assembler, Relief	74	3.7	40.5	3.0
Programmer	69	4.4	42.2	3.2
Cont In Flow	67	11.9	40.8	4.4
Assembly Worker (paced)	63	1.3	41.1	4.0

Source: Adapted from Caplan, et al. (1980).

Table 7.6

Rankings of Support Filters for Occupational Stress

Occupation	(1) Flexibility	(2) Participation	(3) Support from Others	(4) Support at Home	(5) Job Fit
Administrative Professor	2	1	1	1	1
Professor	1	4	6	2	5
Physician	6	13	2	9	2
Administrator	7	2	9	7	11
Supervisor Blue Collar	15	5	16	11	9
Supervisor White Collar	9	3	8	4	18
Scientist	3	8	9	16	13
Air Traffic Controller	11	7	7	14	20
Air Traffic Controller (small airport)	13	6	3	3	21
Train Dispatcher	22	10	18	11	3
Electronic Technician	8	15	9	21	18
Police Officer	13	17	5	5	16
Forklift Driver	23	20	20	14	6
Courier	20	19	17	9	15
Engineer	5	11	15	18	16
Machine Tender	20	23	22	7	4
Tool & Die Worker	18	14	13	22	14
Accountant	10	16	12	11	10
Programmer	4	8	13	19	21
Cont In Flow	11	12	4	6	23
Assembly Worker (paced)	17	22	21	17	7
Assembly Worker (nonpaced)	19	18	19	23	11
Assembler, Relief	16	21	23	19	8

Source: Adapted from Caplan, et al. (1980).

However, here's the good news for chairs. Compared to the other 22 professions (Table 7.6), academic administrators ranked second on personal flexibility (Column 1), and first in the level of participation with others in decisions (Column 2), social support from others at work (Column 3) and spouse, friends and relatives (Column 4). Chairs were also highest in job fit (Column 5) and lowest in job boredom. In essence, they have built in some resistance and resilience to stress attacks, and can never be accused of being bored!

Are You Type A?

But you are still wondering if you are Type A, right? Answer the questions in Exercise 7.2 to see. Better yet, ask your spouse, secretary or closest colleague to answer the questions for you. Assessing your own personality is seldom accurate. True Type A's deny the existence of these traits.

Exercise 7.2
Type Your Behavior

Answer the following questions by indicating what *most often* applies to you:

Yes	No	
_____	_____	1. Do you feel compelled to do most things in a hurry?
_____	_____	2. Are you usually the first one through during a meal?
_____	_____	3. Is it difficult for you to relax, even for a few hours?
_____	_____	4. Do you hate to wait in line at a restaurant, bank, or store?
_____	_____	5. Do you frequently try to do several things at the same time?
_____	_____	6. Are you generally dissatisfied with what you have accomplished in life?
_____	_____	7. Do you enjoy competition and feel you always have to win?
_____	_____	8. When other people speak slowly do you find your self trying to rush them along by finishing the sentence for them?

Yes	No	
_____	_____	9. Do you become impatient when someone does the job slowly?
_____	_____	10. When engaged in conversation do you usually feel compelled to tell others about your own interests?
_____	_____	11. Do you become irritated when something is not done exactly right?
_____	_____	12. Do you rush through your tasks to get them done as quickly as possible?
_____	_____	13. Do you feel you are constantly under pressure to get more done?
_____	_____	14. In the past few years, have you taken less than your allotted vacation time?
_____	_____	15. While listening to other people, do you usually find your mind wandering to other tasks and subjects?
_____	_____	16. When you meet aggressive people do you usually feel compelled to compete with them?
_____	_____	17. Do you tend to talk fast?
_____	_____	18. Are you too busy with your job to have time for hobbies and outside activities?
_____	_____	19. Do you seek and need recognition from your boss and peers?
_____	_____	20. Do you take pride in working best "under pressure"?

```
|     A1     |     A2     |   B1   |   B2   |
20  18   16   14   12   10   8    6    4    2    0
           Number of "Yes" answers
```

Source: Gmelch, W. H. (1982). *Beyond Stress to Effective Management.*

As you probably concluded from the exercise, few individuals fall into either extreme as purely A or B. If you have classified yourself as an A, do not let this alone cause you to return to the less Type A faculty status. There are many techniques available to assist you in becoming shades of Type B, if you choose.

Coping With Type A Behavior

Since coping is an individual art, some of the following techniques will work for you and others will not. Test them and others until you develop your own approach to a more positive perceptual focus (Stage II).

1. *Plan some personal time each day.* Don't operate from a crisis position. Schedule your day to encourage a more positive attitude. Plan a little idleness into each day. Each morning arrive at the office a little early to set the stage for the day before the onslaught of interruptions, demands and conflicts. At noon, make sure you take a mid-day break and have lunch with a colleague or engage in vigorous exercise to cut the eight-to-five stress cycle. Although this may sound unrealistic, leave the office a half hour late in the evening in order to plan the next day and possibly avoid rush-hour traffic.

2. *Compartmentalize chair and non-chair activities.* One of the most difficult tasks for chairs to perform is separating administrative and scholarly activities. A more open approach to work demands is facilitated by compartmentalizing or separating your administrative and your academic duties; it is essential that you make this distinction. Similarly you should separate work (professional) from non-work (personal) activities in order to have higher quality, guilt-free evenings and weekends.

3. *Do one task at a time.* A typical Type A chair eats, walks, works and talks, all at the same time, engaging in what has been termed polyphasic behavior—that is, doing two or more things simultaneously. You can effectively only do one thing at a time, so select the most important task, whether it be administrative, academic or personal, and do it first.

4. *Strive to enrich yourself: physically, socially, mentally and emotionally.* A survey of 4,000 executives found that less than 40 percent have any meaningful activity outside of work. Changing your perceptual focus requires activity and interest in more than one single area. Therefore you need to take a holistic approach toward personal enrichment through selected combinations of physical exercise, social interaction, mental stimulation and emotional stability.

5. *Have a retreat away from the office.* Every chair should have some place where he or she can be alone. You need to be able to get away, close the door and think without interruption—without faculty and staff making demands on your time and attention.

6. *Live by your calendar, not your watch.* Of the stressors faced by chairs, none is as pervasive as time. Break into your fragmented administrative life by setting time aside daily for organizing and planning. Rather than rushing around by the minute hand of your watch, let your weekly calendar dictate your pace.

The stress of being a department chair is what you make of it. That can be the difference between coping and collapsing. The secret of success is not avoiding stressors in Stage I but challenging them with a more positive perceptual response in Stage II. Whether you are exhausted or relaxed, under constant pressure or well-paced, depends on how you approach the stress of crisis. Your personality, outlook and perception can all work to either resist or intensify your stress. Are you thriving in your position, or is your personality killing you? Only you can tell.

THE COPING RESPONSE: STAGE III

While the general literature on coping is significant in volume and diverse in attention, the exact coping process is elusive. Researchers from the disciplines of medicine, psychiatry, clinical psychology, behavioral science and education have undertaken studies to understand the phenomenon of stress and the coping responses.

The foremost authority on stress, Hans Selye, pointed out that despite everything that has been written and said about stress and coping, there is not a ready-made formula that will suit everyone (1974). Since no one technique will suit everyone, how can department chairs positively respond to the stress traps identified in Stage I of the Stress Cycle? The first step, of course, is to develop a more positive "perceptual awareness" to drive the search for effective coping techniques. When faced with such a dilemma, academic chairs might attempt to conceive a technology to control it. Once enough information about a stressor is generated, the tendency is to transform it into a prescription and control it. However, a prescriptive approach may not be an appropriate technology for coping. Blueprints for exact techniques are not available to chairs. One could even assert that coping is an art, not a science, and therefore should be personalized.

Some researchers have attempted to prescribe effective and ineffective techniques which have resulted in misleading conclusions and advice. Others approach coping with singular trend techniques such as relaxation, aerobics, biofeedback, or other such stress interventions. When developing a coping strategy, consider the following propositions as a basis for your response to stress.

1. The individual is the most important variable; no single coping technique is effective for all department chairs in all colleges and universities. Therefore, coping techniques must be sensitive to cultural, social, psychological, and environmental differences in individuals.

2. Individuals can't change the world around them, and chairs cannot change all the barriers in higher education, but they can change how they relate to them.

3. Individuals who cope best develop a repertoire of techniques to counteract different stressors in different situations. This repertoire of techniques should represent a holistic approach toward coping.

How Chairs Cope With Stress

Are there identifiable categories of coping, which, if used holistically, can help department chairs systematically address the stress of academic administration? In answer to this question we asked 800 department chairs: "Recognizing that being a chair is demanding, what ways have you found useful in handling the pressures of your job?" (Gmelch, et al., 1992). The majority of chairs cited more than one response. In all, they identified over 887 coping responses. Content analysis of these responses revealed coping techniques grouped into seven categories. Rather than prescribe specific techniques, review the following categories to see which ones are part of your repertoire.

1. *Social Support.* Chairs indicated social support activities helped them break out of stress traps. They suggest such coping responses as:

- having lunch with colleagues;
- talking it out with a trusted friend;
- sharing frustrations with spouse;
- complaining to other chairs about similar problems;
- consulting with the dean;
- developing companionship with friends outside the department;
- chatting informally with faculty at coffee breaks;
- developing a good working relationship with faculty, staff and students;
- sharing problems with former chairpersons;
- confiding in the office staff;
- relying on advice of selected colleagues;
- having a couple of confidants;
- participating in community activities;
- consoling students and colleagues;
- spending leisure time with family; and
- talking to myself a lot.

2. *Physical Activities.* Chairs reported that the following physical activities helped break the stress cycle: individual sports such as jogging, swimming, walking, hiking, horseback riding, martial arts, golf, skiing and sailing, as well as the team sports of tennis, racquetball and basketball. Many suggested structuring regular physical workouts. Many universities and colleges resemble resorts with all the sports and physical exercise facilities anyone could envision in a vacation resort. The key is to find time to take advantage of them.

3. *Intellectual Stimulation.* Within the third category, intellectual stimulation, chairs cited:

- attending professional conferences;
- reading biographies of political and military personalities;
- the satisfaction of writing manuscripts;
- staying active in, and setting aside time to concentrate on,

research ("at least one day a week, for without it I would go crazy");

- getting out of the office for field work or going to the library;
- teaching at least once a year; and
- enjoying cultural events such as plays and art exhibits.

4. *Entertainment.* The fourth category encompasses entertainment and includes:

- watching television;
- going to a movie or out to dinner;
- getting out of town;
- taking a vacation, mini vacations, or weekend vacation;
- listening to classical music;
- reading novels;
- pondering "Who's Afraid of Virginia Woolf"; and
- attending concerts, art events, and such.

5. *Personal Interests.* The fifth category consists of personal interest techniques such as playing a musical instrument, gardening, gourmet cooking, taking a nature hike, working on arts or crafts, creative writing, taking avocational classes, and other personal hobbies unrelated to work. Some cited just plain "dropping out of sight."

6. *Self-Management.* Chairs identified a proliferation of self-management techniques they used to cope with the pressures including:

- delegating authority to faculty and staff;
- using committees to share the workload;
- involving faculty in decisions;
- planning strategically;
- being assertive and saying no;
- being fair, open and honest;
- listening more than talking;
- scheduling time off for self;

- retreating to one's lab or private office;
- setting goals (and never make department chair the final goal in one's career!);
- being realistic about goals;
- prioritizing work by keeping eyes on goals;
- clearing the desk every day;
- effectively and efficiently using time;
- building in time for other interests;
- keeping communication open with faculty;
- building trust with colleagues;
- hiring competent staff;
- asking for help from department members;
- reserving inviolable blocks of time for family and research;
- keeping separate the life as a researcher and as a chair;
- hibernating to work on activities requiring intense concentration;
- partying whenever possible or having a quiet social life;
- dealing with conflict constructively; and
- having an excellent, dedicated secretary and administrative staff.

7. *Supportive Attitudes.* Finally, chairs identified numerous coping techniques which could be categorized simply as supportive attitudes. They cited such attitudinal techniques as:

   - being optimistic and keeping a positive outlook;
   - developing a sense of humor (plus a profound Marxist—Groucho—philosophy);
   - going home guilt-free (even if it means late!);
   - emotionally distancing oneself from the job (leave the worry at the workplace—nothing goes home except me!);
   - don't take on others' anxieties;
   - depersonalizing issues;

- being patient;
- minimizing self-importance;
- knowing one's limitations;
- laughing;
- crying; and
- recognizing that some stress is normal.

While not one of the responses taken separately presents *the* answer to coping, taken collectively chairs can view this as a coping taxonomy from which to seek their own stress reduction.

Coping with stress is a holistic proposition. It is much like weight loss, if one were to exercise more, but eat more too, the results may not be as beneficial as exercising more while cutting back or stabilizing one's diet. In much the same way, effective coping consists of building a repertoire of techniques equally balanced in the social, physical, intellectual, entertainment, managerial, personal and attitudinal categories. Your goal is to reduce your stress by adding some of these techniques to your present repertoire of stress responses. It is not the chair who masters one technique that copes most effectively and creatively, but the one who possesses the flexibility to call upon any number of techniques from various sources—physical activity, managerial skills, social support, and so on.

The holistic coping effect becomes synergistic, providing physical, emotional and intellectual benefits. Only you can make the final decision. Each chair has his or her own tastes, time schedules and preferences. Some chairs find certain techniques, like luncheon therapy sessions once a week with other chairs, more helpful than dining alone. The authors of this book realized that their sedentary administrative practices added not only stress to their lives but weight onto their frames so they pledged to get involved in racquetball three times a week. Not only do we now report less stress, but have trimmed off a few pounds and benefitted from sharper mental acuity. You must discover for yourself the activities most agreeable to you in each of the coping categories—but remember, the answer is in the holistic approach to stress reduction. No matter what the activities, take it slow and easy. Just go quietly, keep it personal, and you will have a good chance of success.

FROM ILLNESS TO WELLNESS—CONSEQUENCES: STAGE IV

Behind the achievements of many great academics lies the factor of stress. Based on a study of 1,200 faculty members, Figure 7.2 shows how stress interacted with their productivity (Wilke, Gmelch & Lovrich, 1985). A moderate amount of stress helped them reach peak performance; however when stress reached "excessive" proportions (burnout), their performance significantly declined. Note also that without sufficient stress (lack of motivation or challenge— rustout), their performance also declined.

Figure 7.2
Stress and Performance

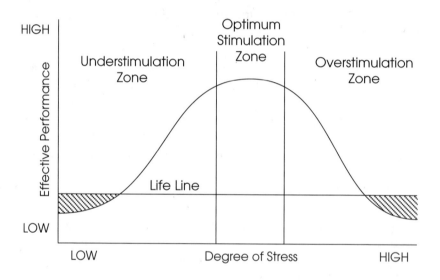

Department chairs often experience excessive stress. After all, they can only put out so many brush fires before eventually burning out themselves. It is at this point that stress becomes a most powerful and elusive enemy, playing a major role in a variety of illnesses. By proper management of the Chair Stress Cycle, the end result of stress should not be illness but wellness. Your stress cycle can be a positive, upward spiral toward wellness if you are able to manage your stressors in Stage I, reinforce your resilient personality in Stage II, and develop a repertoire of positive coping techniques in Stage III. You can then achieve wellness to the point where you no longer seek treatment. That is, you are free of signs, symptoms and disabilities of illness. But this does not necessarily mean that you are well. In order to climb to wellness you must go beyond, into the preventative, holistic side and build up your strength through a variety of stress-reduction practices.

Department Chair Action Plan

The following Chair Action Plan suggests dividing stressors into two categories: (1) those internally controlled and (2) those externally beyond one's control. Those within your control should be managed at the cause level by self-management techniques. Those beyond your control should be attacked at the symptom level with stress absorbers such as relaxation, nutrition, exercise and coping attitudes.

The majority of top stressors identified in the research on department chairs and from your results in Exercise 7.1 (Chair Stress Inventory), most likely relate directly to (a) time, (b) administrative tasks, (c) academic endeavors, and (d) personal expectations. Clearly some of these stressors are more controllable than others. Most chairs would agree that they could become better managers of their time and personal expectations, but it is more difficult to change salaries and other organizational constraints in such difficult economic and administrative times.

Therefore the key to stress reduction rests with a wise old adage: we should seek "the courage to change the things we can, the serenity to accept those we cannot, and the wisdom to know the difference." In other words, you need to identify the causes of chair stress that you can control and resolve them. Those that are inherent in your job and cannot be controlled, you must learn to live with and absorb the pressure. Attack the symptoms rather than the causes.

Alternatively, the first and most critical step in controlling your stress is to take charge of the stressors you have identified in Exercise 7.1. The Chair Action Plan in Exercise 7.3 will help you successfully reduce these menacing stressors. The purpose of the plan is to systematically dissect and redirect stressors by analyzing the *causes* of each stressor, examining potential *solutions*, and finally taking corrective *actions*. Specifically, the steps of the Chair Action Plan are:.

1. Identify a bothersome *stressor* over which you have some control;

2. Search for the *causes* of the stressful event;

3. Generate a set of possible *solutions* to remedy the causes;

4. Specify a *plan* to alleviate the cause;

5. Develop a *timetable* to implement the plan;

6. Set a date and method of *follow-up* and evaluate the effectiveness of the plan; and

7. Investigate potential problems or *unintended consequences* the plan may have created (Gmelch, 1982).

Exercise 7.3
Chair Action Plan

I. Most bothersome stress event: _____

II. CAUSES	III. SOLUTIONS	IV. SPECIFIC ACTION PLAN
1.	1.	a. The plan is to:
2.	2.	
3.	3.	
4.	4.	
5.	5.	

V. STEPS FOR IMPLEMENTATION	
1. Activity:	3. How often:
2. Where:	4. When:

VI. FOLLOW-UP EVALUATION	
1.	3.
2.	4.

VII. NEGATIVE UNINTENDED CONSEQUENCES	
1.	3.
2.	4.

© Gmelch, W. H. (1982). *Beyond Stress to Effective Management.*

While the Chair Action Plan may be seen as mechanical and systematic, its logic is exactly what makes it work. An example is shown in Figure 7.3 of a completed worksheet examining the problem of "too heavy a workload." Eliminating the cause is the only way to truly alleviate stress.

Figure 7.3
Chair Action Plan — "Heavy Workload"

I. Most bothersome stress event: <u>Too heavy a work load, one that cannot be finished in a day</u>

II. CAUSES	III. SOLUTIONS	IV. SPECIFIC ACTION PLAN
1. Unrealistic appraisal of time	1. Conduct time schedules	a. The plan is to: Concentrate on high payoff tasks
2. Inability to say "no"	2. Gain assertive skills	b. Type of action
3. Overcommitted to family	3. Set family/job goals	☒ corrective ☐ interim
4. Unclear delineation of responsibilities	4. Request specific Faculty Planning Guide	☐ adaptive ☐ preventive
5. Cannot distinguish between high and low priorities	5. Concentrate on high	☐ contingent

V. STEPS FOR IMPLEMENTATION

1. Activity: Develop high payoff and low payoff lists	3. How often: Daily for two weeks
2. Where: In the office at my desk with no interruptions	4. When: Every morning at 8:30 a.m.

VI. FOLLOW-UP EVALUATION

1. Did I write out my lists every morning?	3. Did I actually delegate or eliminate any low payoff tasks?
2. Were the high payoff tasks completed first?	4.

VII. NEGATIVE UNINTENDED CONSEQUENCES

1. My dean became upset with incomplete tasks important to him/her	3. I created an overload for my staff by delegating too many tasks to them
2. Work became too regimented and not as carefree	4.

***MODIFICATIONS OF PLAN NEEDED? Since my dean needs to know what I am concentrating on (high payoffs), I should communicate with him/her periodically to seek concurrence with my plan.

For those stressors beyond your control, three other steps are needed to absorb the pressure. Exercise, proper nutrition and relaxation represent these critical steps to stress control. These will provide you with a sound body and mind to repel the onslaught of daily tensions and frustrations. Together with the holistic coping techniques in Stage III, you can have a full range of stress reduction techniques, from managing to making, from solving the problems to absorbing the symptoms.

The Chair-Staff Team

No department is complete without considering the most important element in any chair's performance—the chair-staff team. This team strategy differs slightly from that of the previous chair suggestions. First, many staff stressors have different causes than the department chair's. In fact, the most significant stressor may be the chair! For example, a study of over 200 education office staff members reveals their most bothersome activities as:

1. being interrupted frequently by telephone calls and drop-in visitors;

2. waiting to get information needed to carry out job duties;

3. imposing excessively high self-expectations;

4. too heavy a workload, one that cannot be finished during the normal work day;

5. too little authority to carry out responsibilities;

6. being treated as less important by professors and chairs;

7. working in a noisy, disruptive environment;

8. needing to see the chair and not being able to;

9. trying to get the chair to complete reports and other paperwork on time; and

10. being bored by routine tasks.

A comparison of staff stressors with those of chairs reveals a few common themes on which they can work together (interruptions, paperwork, heavy workload and excessively high self-expectations). For example, chairs could be most helpful to their support staff simply by: giving them access to schedules, policies and other important information; ensuring that faculty treat staff as professionals; providing information in a timely fashion; and breaking up boring, routine tasks. Also, just because colleges and universities typically do not encourage and support inservice training does not mean that you cannot send your office staff to workshops and seminars to hone their skills and attack their secretarial stressors. Professional growth and development provides the foundation for departmental productivity.

COPING WITH CHAIR STRESS TRAPS

No amount of research can provide the single answer on how to cope with chair stress problems. However, the following suggestions reinforce strategies suggested in Chapters Five and Six which are also helpful in attacking the general sources of department chair stress.

Managing Management Time

The paperwork, meetings, deadlines and workload represent not the ends of managerial and academic productivity but the means to important goals in higher education. Therefore, you should incorporate and practice a few other time management principles, in addition to those already suggested in Chapter Five.

1. Identify high pay-off (HIPO) activities (most important, not urgent) which will help attain excellence in both management and faculty responsibilities. For example, budget, personnel, and personal productivity activities should take precedence over administrative details, unimportant meetings, filing unread reports, and answering meaningless correspondence.

2. Reduce the involvement of chairs in less meaningful, low pay-off (LOPO) processes. This is the corollary of the first principle. You can find more time for HIPO's if you delegate or eliminate your LOPO's. The key for chairs, however, is to identify the LOPO's so they can be ignored—a difficult task for most managers since everything they do seems so important.

3. Develop a more efficient working environment so that routine paperwork can be handled by office assistants; telephone calls can be screened; time can be blocked into uninterruptible periods for productive, thoughtful work;

and when possible, a HIPO hideout can be used as a retreat to prepare manuscripts and keep up with the academic discipline.

Productive Conflict Resolution

As you discovered in Chapter Six, the chairperson's most frequent and serious conflict arises in confronting peers, and on occasion, the dean. A few reminders may be helpful in working with your colleagues and dean:

1. The power of the chair does not rest as much in the position (power of reward and punishment) as it does in the person (influence by referent, expertise, and collegiality). Therefore, use your position power sparingly and build a solid personal power base with your dean and faculty members by working with them in an open, honest and professional manner.

2. When caught between the demands of administration and the needs of faculty, explore common interests that transcend and satisfy both parties.

3. Work on getting faculty involved and having them buy into the solutions—your role is more to facilitate than direct.

Enabling Constraints

While rules and regulations restrict chairs' flexibility and cause unwanted stress, do not be discouraged by rules alone. They merely represent boundaries around a pasture within which you and the department can operate. Understand the boundaries and be creative about how to reach goals and objectives while staying within the pasture.

Academic Productivity

Have you become a role prisoner of faculty productivity pressures and administrative challenges? The study of department chairs reveals that their number one stressor is trying to keep current in their discipline. In addition, preparing manuscripts for publication and maintaining academic career progress also rank in the top ten chair stress traps. In essence, department chairs have become role prisoners of both faculty productivity pressures and administrative leadership challenges. If you follow the same pattern, protect your time and resources by maintaining an Academic Protection Plan.

1. Block uninterrupted periods of time to engage in thoughtful scholarly activities.

2. Maintain another office on campus or at home to ensure that an equivalent of a half-to-a-full day a week can be devoted to your academic endeavors.

3. Establish a research or writing team of faculty members and/or graduate students.

4. Negotiate a sabbatical between terms or at the end of the term to regain currency in the discipline.

Any approach to reducing chair stress rests both with the chair's willingness to seek creative solutions and the institution's responsiveness to develop effective and productive leadership. While the future for academic leadership may appear rife with stress, it is also replete with challenges and creative opportunities.

8

LEADERSHIP TRADE-OFFS AND PAY-OFFS

Clearly then, we cannot do away with specialization, nor would we wish to. But in the modern world it has extended far beyond anything we knew in the past....there are many tasks that can be effectively performed only by men and women who have retained some capacity to function as generalists—leadership and management...
> — *John W. Gardner*

For many academics, work has become their entire life. Over 60 percent of administrators have nothing of greater meaning in their lives than work—and since chairs work an average of 55 hours per week, over half of their waking hours are consumed by work. Work and the role of chair give an identity and self-concept that often dictate who you socialize with, where you live, how long you live there, and what lifestyle you lead. Obviously, administration plays an important part in your life and provides you with pleasures as well as pressures.

What price do you pay for your venture into administration? Where will it lead? What are the benefits? And what leadership challenges do you foresee in your future? The answers to these and other questions regarding the challenges of leadership are addressed in this chapter.

LEADERSHIP TRADE-OFFS

Your ability to develop a holistic managerial lifestyle depends on how well you make trade-offs between your professional and personal time and interests.

A personal or professional trade-off is defined as *an exchange of one interest in return for another; especially, a giving up of something desirable* (Greiff & Munther, 1980). In essence, life is a trade-off, yet success depends in large measure on making effective trade-offs. In the case of being a department chair, have you been able to keep a balance among your academic, administrative and personal roles? Or do you perceive that you have accepted the leadership challenge at the expense of your professorial pleasures and personal enjoyments?

Assuming the position of department chair raises four central questions that will impact the degree to which your tradeoffs are effective (Gmelch, 1991): (1) Have you been able to continue professional and personal activities you enjoyed before becoming chair? (2) If your time has shifted significantly among faculty, managerial and personal activities, are you satisfied with these changes? (3) What stresses and pressures were created when you assumed the chair position? (4) What impact will this leadership change have on your professional career?

The first part of this chapter addresses trade-offs in becoming department chair and using these trade-offs to find a more holistic balance in your life. It illuminates the "dark side" of the department chair position. The intention is not to discourage you from continuing to seek the challenges of academic leadership, but help you recognize, prepare for, and overcome unforeseen trade-offs. The conclusion of this chapter highlights the positive side of the position and identifies the pay-offs to give balance to your professional life.

TRADE-OFFS: BALANCING TIME AND STRESS

One of the prices professors must pay when they enter the chair position is time commitment. Since time is inelastic and irreplaceable, one must trade some faculty or personal time for newly acquired administrative duties. Keep your career in mind as you consider department chair trade-offs as outlined in Figure 8.1 and elaborated below.

Figure 8.1
Properties of Trade-Offs

1. Trade-offs are like a ledger

2. Trade-offs vie for the same resources

3. Trade-offs create dissatisfaction

4. Trade-offs create an imbalance and lead to stress

5. Trade-off decisions favor the urgent

6. Trade-offs change with age and position

7. Trade-offs cannot always be controlled

8. Trade-off consequences cannot always be predicted

9. Trade-off conflicts can be reduced by separation of private and professional goals

10. Trade-offs favor one side or the other—unless goals are established

The Department Chair's Ten Trade-Offs

1. *Trade-offs act much like a ledger, a chair cannot debit one side without crediting the other.* As professors assume the chair position, the credits added to the administrative side of the ledger must be debited against certain faculty activities. In other words, the chair position comes at some cost to faculty time since time resembles a "zero-sum" game—everyone has 24 hours in a day, no less and no more.

   In order to gain personal insight into how you handle time changes from the move to chair, try the Personal and Professional Time Audit in Exercise 8.1.

   Just as you responded to Exercise 8.1, hundreds of department chairs in the Center for the Study of the Department Chair (see Preface for details) were asked whether they had spent more, the same, or less time in professional and personal activities since they became chairs. Table 8.1 reveals a dramatic shift from time spent in professional activities of research and writing, keeping current in their discipline, and teaching. Chairs reported spending 88 percent, 82 percent and 56 percent less time in these activities, respectively. The reduction in time spent was not as pronounced but included the

Exercise 8.1
Personal and Professional Time Audit

Since you became department chair do you have more, the same, or less time in the following categories? Please indicate whether you are satisfied with this time allocation.

	amount of time			Are you satisfied with this time allocation?	
	More	Same	Less	Yes	No
Personal					
Family	☐	☐	☐	☐	☐
Friends	☐	☐	☐	☐	☐
Leisure time	☐	☐	☐	☐	☐
Spiritual time	☐	☐	☐	☐	☐
Civic activities	☐	☐	☐	☐	☐
Professional					
Research/writing	☐	☐	☐	☐	☐
Remaining current in discipline	☐	☐	☐	☐	☐
Teaching	☐	☐	☐	☐	☐
Service	☐	☐	☐	☐	☐
Contact with students	☐	☐	☐	☐	☐
Contact with colleagues and friends in your institution	☐	☐	☐	☐	☐
Contact with colleagues and friends outside your institution	☐	☐	☐	☐	☐

other professional areas of "service" and "contact with students and colleagues inside and outside of the institutions." What has been your shift in professional time?

2. *Trade-offs between professional and personal interests vie for the same resource—time.* The second part of Table 8.1 shows an almost equally pronounced percent of chairs reduced their personal time with family (65 percent), friends (56 percent) and leisure (77 percent) due to administrative duties. Spiritual and civic activities interestingly enough remained "the same" for most chairs. Have you had less time for your family,

Table 8.1
Professor to Department Chair:
Percent Change in Use of Time

	More Time (Credit)	Less Time (Debit)	Same Time (No Change)
A. **Professional Time**			
1. Research and writing	2%	88%	9%
2. Current in discipline	2%	82%	15%
3. Teaching	4%	78%	18%
4. Service	35%	25%	38%
5. Student contact	20%	49%	29%
6. Inside colleague contact	34%	28%	42%
7. Outside colleague contact	16%	38%	44%
B. **Personal Time**			
1. Family	2%	65%	33%
2. Friends	1%	56%	41%
3. Leisure time	1%	77%	22%
4. Civic activities	7%	38%	53%

friends and leisure activities since assuming your chair responsibilities?

3. *Trade-offs can create dissatisfaction with personal and professional lives.* This property of trade-offs becomes even more important when you consider your satisfaction with shifts in your time (refer back to Exercise 8.1). Chairs were asked if they were satisfied with their shift in time allocations. As Figure 8.2 portrays, of those chairs who spent less time in certain activities, an overwhelming percent expressed dissatisfaction with debiting their time in scholarly writing and research (87.5 percent) and keeping current in their discipline (94 percent), as well as their personal loss of time with family (89 percent), friends (87.5 percent) and leisure (79.5 percent). As an aside, over 80 percent of the chairs in this study believed that "their loads should be lightened to make more time for research, writing or other work in the field," and that "if no

opportunity were available to do personal research (they) would find the job less satisfying." Ironically, those chairs who spent less time teaching were split: 55 percent satisfied and 45 percent dissatisfied with their reduced teaching loads. Are you dissatisfied with the shifts that have occurred in your time allocations?

4. *Too many trade-offs in one direction create an imbalance and lead to negative stress.* This trade-off illuminates another price paid for leadership: excessive stress. Is your position as chair a major contributor of the stress in your life? Take a minute and indicate on the scale below what you perceive the percent of the total stress in your life results from being a chair.

0% ··········25% ···········50%············75% ···········100%

When this question was asked of 1,600 department chairs across the United States (Center for the Study of the Department Chair, 1990, 1992), they perceived that 70 percent of the stress in their lives came from their job. Chairs seem to be trapped between the pressures and demands of performing not only as administrators, but also as productive faculty members. The academic versus administrator role paradox is a common song of despair chairs sing, and is reconfirmed when chairs' most serious stressors are compared with those of faculty. For example, almost 60 percent of the chairs suffered from "heavy workloads" compared to 40 percent of the professors. Overall, chairs experience more stress than faculty. Not only do they seem to retain many of the highest faculty stressors while holding the chair position, they also add such managerial stressors as confrontation with colleagues, new time demands, and institutional constraints (Gmelch and Burns, 1993).

5. *Routine trade-off decisions usually favor the urgent over the important.* Daily pressures and stresses usually result in the tyranny of the urgent. Although urgent, these tasks may not represent the important points of your job. Due to the sense of urgency they receive immediate attention, leaving important responsibilities in imbalance. For example, correspondence that has to beat the two o'clock mail pick-up takes priority but sometimes at the expense of a waiting faculty member. If typing a

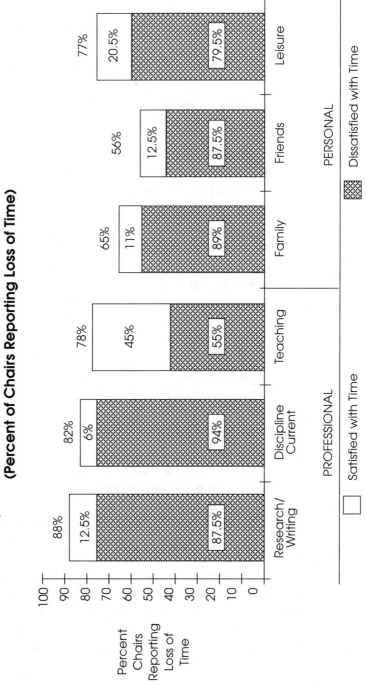

Figure 8.2
Satisfaction of Department Chairs with Less Time for Professional and Personal Activities
(Percent of Chairs Reporting Loss of Time)

memo to the graduate school is really important, perhaps a quick telephone call instead of the memo could meet the emergency, save an appointment with a faculty member, and keep you in balance.

In the same spirit, many relatively unimportant tasks creep into your personal time unless you protect your calendar. Just as you take your professional calendar home and announce time commitments to your family and friends, you should also take your personal calendar to work and protect your personal commitments. For example, season tickets to plays, performances and sports events should be written on your work calendar so you can protect their times and dates.

6. *Trade-offs change with age, position, tenure, maturity, health and time.* Think back to your first assignment as department chair. The scales usually tip in favor of the managerial role (filing reports on time, writing memos, etc.) until one becomes established in the new position. Only after you begin to settle in and adapt to what you believe is most important in your role as chair do you become comfortable in your position. Of course, this will change over time and experience in the position.

Does this identity and interest in academic administration significantly change over your tenure as chair? As we showed in Chapter One, 46 percent of the chairs would serve again, 30 percent would not, and 24 percent were still undecided.

As you think about how you may have changed since you traded your faculty job for the chair position, ask yourself today, Who am I? A faculty member? An administrator? Or, both faculty and administrator? In answer to this question, our 1992 study disclosed that almost 60 percent of chairs considered themselves as professor, another 22 percent as administrator and the remaining fifth (19 percent) suffered from the ambiguity of filling the roles of both professor and administrator. Evidently, many professors who become chairs never completely identify with the leadership position. After all, they typically spend a couple of decades in their discipline as doctoral students and through the ranks of professorship before becoming department chairs. Due to this long socialization process, many department chairs never make the full trade-off, thus, they willingly return to faculty status (at a rate of 65 percent) without any stigma of failure or demotion.

7. *Chairs cannot always control their trade-off decisions.* Deans, faculty, family and friends dictate some rules that become immutable conditions of a chair's life. It is not always possible to trade-off a weekday morning of writing at home for late evenings in the office. Family expect you at home and faculty want you in the office. Nor may noon racquetball games be willingly traded off for administrative luncheon meetings— the dean controls the time and the agenda!

8. *Chairs cannot always predict the consequences of trade-offs.* While the commitment to attend professional conferences and emergency meetings out of town may represent professionally rewarding opportunities, too many absences from the home and office may eventually result in no place to return.

9. *The clearer the distinction and separation between personal and professional goals—and between academic and administrative goals— the less the potential conflict between their trade-offs.* While Chapter Seven primarily focused on resolving the 70 percent stress from administrative sources, you should not ignore the other 30 percent created by pressures away from the job for two important reasons. First, department chair effectiveness depends somewhat on your ability to handle pressures from your private life; and second, managers need to approach their lifestyles holistically, trading-off effectively between their personal and professional goals. In other words, in order to be an effective leader you need to be an effective person— parent, spouse, public servant, colleague and professional. One cannot be unhealthy or ineffective in one's private life and still be an effective manager in one's professional life. In order to succeed you must find the balance between your private and professional needs.

Establish goals in your personal, and academic and administrative lives, and attempt to treat them as separate but equal entities. Exercise 8.2 may help you separate and track your personal and professional responsibilities and activities. If you stack the scale on one side you will short the other, giving neither the balance it deserves.

Exercises 8.2
Balancing Your Trade-offs

List in the boxes below your most important "high-payoff" activities or responsibilities in your personal and professional lives.

Personal	Professional
1.	1.
2.	2.
3.	3.
4.	4.

10. *Trade-off decisions continue to favor one side or the other unless goals are established and updated periodically.* Without personal goals or objectives to guide a chair in making trade-off decisions, the demand of activities dominating one side of the scale can engulf one's energy and time. Lay your goals out for the semester, year, or term of office, rather than itemizing activities on a daily basis. Remember, without balance you may return to faculty status and find that you are sorely outdated in your discipline, or you may reach the end of your professional career to find yourself out of touch with your important personal interests.

In order to prevent the imbalance caused by time, stress and job dissatisfaction, chairs need to perform a number of these balancing acts and create a leadership position which both challenges and satisfies them as scholars serving as academic leaders.

PAY-OFFS: REWARDS OF THE POSITION

Illuminating the "dark side" of the department chair position does not go without highlighting some rewards and benefits. Serving as department chair must have some significant rewards which counterbalance the frustrations. What are they?

Most would say privately that status and prestige come with the position. But to admit to their faculty colleagues that they enjoy the job causes suspicion. As Dressel points out: "A scholar is not expected to seek or enjoy the position of chair" (1970, p. 82). If, in fact, one appears to enjoy the assignment or maintain it for several terms they become suspected of leaving their discipline for the comfort of administration to justify the lack of scholarly contributions (Moses & Roe, 1990). In public chairs are reluctant to admit the pay-offs of administration as it is "unwise, even indecent, because it means one is proclaiming oneself as administrator, whereas most (chairs), especially those on short term appointments are anxious to remain, and to be seen to be, academics rather than administrators (Moses & Roe, 1990, p. 209)." But the chair position is not perceived by many as a career move, rather a temporary service to the institution and profession.

However, in private chairs candidly speak about the rewards they receive. From interviews of 100 department heads in Australia (Moses & Roe, 1990) and two national surveys of 1,600 chairs in the United States (Gmelch, Carroll, Seedorf & Wentz, 1990; Gmelch, Burns, Carroll, Harris & Wentz, 1992) chairs resoundingly testified about the benefits and pay-offs of department leadership. While many of their testimonies overlap, six areas of reward emerge.

Financial Reward

Monetarily, 72 percent of the chairs in our study received an administrative stipend averaging 12 percent of their salary or an average stipend of $3,432. In Australian universities the financial compensation ranged from as little as $360 per annum up to nearly $7,000. While money alone does not seem to motivate professors to become chairs, it does represent a partial pay-off for dealing with the demands of the job. Booth concludes that "the primary source of satisfaction for chairs must come from nonmonetary rewards since their financial stipend is usually modest" (1982, p. 36).

Personal Sense of Achievement

Chairs who derived a sense of personal achievement from their position expressed it this way: "When I see results of my efforts realized," "when I experience a victory," or "when I have the chance to accomplish something positive."

Personal Sense of Power

While similar to personal achievement, satisfaction from the ability to have and exercise power emerged as a separate and distinct motive. Although not readily apparent to some chairs and uneasy and embarrassing to others, many enjoyed the ability to exercise power—especially as it enabled them to direct the department and propagate their own ideas. Their feelings about this satisfaction ranged from the most blatant ("I enjoy power") to the most subtle ("Leading, guiding developments in the department is the reward. I initiated new developments, set it all up, and now I'm enjoying it") (Moses & Roe, 1990, p. 214).

Altruistic Satisfaction

Chairs often spoke of their pleasure in "opening doors of opportunities" and "making the job easier" for others as well as helping them achieve their goals—"made everyone feel good about their own professional development." In a faculty-team sense, they expressed satisfaction with being able to develop a collegial atmosphere where they "increased the level of civility" and "kept the peace without too many serious mistakes."

Departmental Success

Chairs also received great satisfaction from building a quality program by "creating a pathway to a stronger department through strategic planning." Some chairs used the seaworthy captain analogy by expressing the satisfaction of maintaining their programs under rough seas: "the ship is still afloat" and "I kept a leaking life boat afloat without throwing anyone to the sharks." Others simply said they "held the fort," "kept the place from falling apart" and "maintained a high quality program in a time of major financial crisis."

Personal Growth

Many chairs expressed gratitude for what the chair position had done for them. They learned on their job and received a broader perspective from which to view the college, university and educational environment as well as had the opportunity to test some of their "latent" leadership skills. Approximately 20 percent of chairs used their experience to move into higher levels of administration. While most expressed satisfaction with their personal growth opportunities, it must also be remembered that 65 percent of the chairs did return to faculty status after serving as chair (Carroll, 1990).

On a positive note, Tucker (1984) highlights the psychic rewards of being a department chair:

> ...there is the personal satisfaction derived from helping others with their professional development and from helping to guide and build an effective academic program. There is the challenge of leadership, which many people find invigorating. They find rewards in guiding the guiders of students, shaping curricula, defending the interests of the department, and interacting with other academic leaders, including deans and vice-presidents. Many have come to feel that their ability to motivate others to greatness perhaps exceeds their ability to motivate themselves. Some of these chairpersons want to enhance their administrative effectiveness by developing whatever additional skills are necessary to implement the management process. Some chairpersons see the acquisition of such skills as a prerequisite for further advancement in academic administration. (p. 389)

DID YOU MAKE A DIFFERENCE?

Chairs normally serve six years, after which they typically follow one of two paths. Approximately one-in-five chairs move upward in academic administration and complete the full transition from faculty to administration. However, most chairs do not continue in administration, but return to faculty status where they remain until retirement. "Like the springtime observations of wildflowers and dormant creatures, there is a sense of a natural, undirected process at work....The life cycle of chairs is emerging from faculty, being active briefly in the leadership of the institution and department, and returning to the faculty in a more dormant leadership state" (Carroll, 1990, p. 117).

This metaphor may be an accurate portrayal of department leadership. Inevitably all chairs leave their positions. Is your destiny back to scholarship or on to higher levels of management? Before you leave, you may want to reflect on whether you made a difference. You may find it interesting to answer the following question: When you leave the chair position, what do you hope others in your department will think you have accomplished?

Write Your Epitaph

Hundreds of chairs from our studies reflected on this question and collectively viewed their accomplishments in the following light.

Productive Climate. Chairs wanted to be known for developing a sense of academic excitement, providing faculty with opportunity for gratification and satisfaction, enhancing faculty's professional life, reducing the stress on faculty, and restoring peace and fostering growth among faculty.

Collegial Atmosphere. Many chairs hoped their faculty felt an improved sense of collegiality where conflicts could be healed, the level of civility was increased, morale was enhanced, and some peace and order was brought to the department.

Program Advancement. Many chairs aspired to build a national program, bring the department into the 21st Century, focus the department area of concentration, enhance the department's reputation, increase the department's status within the university, upgrade the department's teaching and research, build better relations with the field, and modernize the curriculum and physical facilities.

Quality Staffing. Many chairs wanted to leave their legacy by recruiting and developing competent faculty, especially by promoting women and minorities and nurturing young faculty members.

Quality Leadership. Chairs reflected on their personal qualities and hoped they would be respected for their honesty, openness, fairness, justice and altruism. They also sought to provide the vision and strategic direction needed to advance the mission of the department into the next century. As a summary note, one chair hoped the faculty would say that "he accomplished most of what he said needed to be done, and did it with integrity."

If you had to write your epitaph today, what would it be?

BALANCING STRATEGIES

The final analysis is that the dynamic and changing environments present a leadership crisis in higher education. What is the answer to attracting capable leaders as department chairs? Listed below are a few ideas to make your position more attractive and enjoyable.

Restructure the Position

Work with your dean to reduce the expectations of the position to a half-time assignment. Negotiate proper support to manage the key responsibilities of the position. Besides secretarial support, request a research assistant to the office management team to conduct the necessary reports for the university, state agencies and outside constituencies.

Purge Unnecessary Administrivia

Related to restructuring the position is the need to reduce the amount of paperwork and requests for reports rarely read. Since the highest stress on chairs comes from overload, concentrate on your department's high pay-off activities rather than respond to the urgent, but sometimes not so important. Each request should be measured against its contribution to the department's mission and goals.

Reverse the Hierarchy

Traditionally and structurally universities are top-down hierarchies. Chairs serve at the pleasure of, and for, the dean. You might ask why deans exist. In part, the answer should be to provide support and leadership for department chairs. Be proactive and seek your dean's help. In turn, chairs should serve their faculty, as the faculty serve the students.

Protect Scholarship Interests

Data from our studies confirm that chairs need more time for their scholarly pursuits and personal interests while serving departments. If your time for keeping current in your discipline and research is not protected, you may become dissatisfied and more reluctant to continue as chair. Blocking time for research, maintaining a separate research office, and seeking support for a research assistant while serving as chair will produce a work environment conducive to productive administration and scholarship.

Train for Leadership

It is well known that few chairs receive training to prepare and maintain their skills in leadership. The value of leadership is too great not to invest in the most critical unit in the academic institution. Both managerial skills and leadership perspectives are needed to meet the challenges facing higher education. Table 8.2 lists the areas chairs identify where training is most needed.

Table 8.2
Areas Chairs Indicate Most Need for Training

1. Evaluate faculty performance

2. Maintain conducive work climate (reducing conflicts among faculty)

3. Obtain and manage external funds (grants, contracts)

4. Prepare and propose budgets

5. Develop and initiate long-range departmental goals

6. Manage department resources (finances, facilities, equipment)

7. Encourage professional development activities of faculty

8. Manage non-academic staff

9. Plan and evaluate curriculum development

10. Provide informal faculty leadership

11. Assure the maintenance of accurate departmental records

12. Recruit and select faculty

In order to prevent the possible imbalance created by your leadership role, a number of these ideas can help you restructure your role as department chair. While the future of academic leadership may be plagued by paradoxes inherent in the position, it is also replete with rewards and challenges. This book was written to assist you in understanding your role as department leader and developing the skills necessary to enjoy your faculty, reap the rewards and lead your department into the twenty-first century.

BIBLIOGRAPHY

Alinsky, S. D. (1971). *Rules for radicals: A practical primer for realistic radicals.* New York, NY: Random House.

Andrews, K. R. (1987). *The concept of corporate strategy* (3rd ed.). Homewood, IL: Richard D. Irwin.

Bare, A. (1986). Managerial behavior of college chairpersons and administrators. *Research in Higher Education,* 24(2), 128-138.

Bare, A. C. (1980). The study of academic department performance. *Research in Higher Education,* 12 (1).

Bass, B. M. (1985). *Leadership and performance beyond expectations.* New York, NY: Free Press.

Bennett, J. B. (1983). *Managing the academic department.* Phoenix, AZ: American Council on Education/Oryx.

Bennis, W. G., Benne, K. D. & Chin, R. (1969). *The planning of change* (2nd ed.). New York, NY: Holt, Rhinehart and Winston.

Bennis, W. & Nanus, B. (1985). *Leaders: The strategy for taking charge.* New York, NY: Harper & Row.

Booth, D. B. (1982). *The department chair: Professional development and role conflict.* AAHE-ERIC Higher Education Research Report No. 10. Washington, DC: AAHE.

Bowen, H. R. & Schuster, J. H. (1986). *American professors: A national resource imperiled.* New York, NY: Oxford University Press.

Bradford, D. & Cohen, A. R. (1984). *Managing for excellence.* New York, NY: Wiley.

Brown, T. L. (1988). Putting vision into perspective. *Industry Week,* July 4.

Burns, J. S. (1992). *Dimensions of university academic department chair stress: A national study.* Unpublished doctoral dissertation, Washington State University.

Burns, J. S. & Gmelch, W. H. (1992). *Stress factors, role conflict and role ambiguity for academic department chairs: A national study.* Paper presented at the American Educational Research Association Conference, San Francisco, CA.

Caplan, R. D., Cobb, S., French, J. R. P., Van Harrison,, R. & Pinneau, S. R. (1980). *Job demands and worker health: Main effects and occupational differences.* HEW Publication No. (N10SH), 75-160.

Carroll, J. (1990). *Career paths of department chairs in doctorate-granting institutions.* Unpublished doctoral dissertation, Washington State University.

Chubb, J. E. (!988). Why the current wave of school reform will fail. *The Public Interest,* Winter, 28-49.

Cleveland, H. (1985). *The knowledge executive: Leadership in an information society.* New York, NY: Dutton.

Cope, R. G. (1987). *Opportunity from strength: Strategic planning clarified with case examples,* ASHE-ERIC Higher Education report No. 8. Washington DC: Association for the Study of Higher Education.

Corwin, R. G. (1969). Patterns of organizational conflict. *Administrative Science Quarterly,* December, 507-520.

Creswell, J. W., Wheeler, D. W., Seagren, A. T., Egly, N. J. & Beyer, K. D. (1990). *The academic chairperson's handbook.* Lincoln, NE: The University of Nebraska Press.

DeMeuse, K. P. & Liebowitz, S. J. (1981). An empirical analysis of team building research. *Group & Organization Studies,* 6(3), 357-378.

Diebold, J. (1984). *Making the future work.* New York, NY: Simon & Schuster.

Dillard, C. (1992). *Leadership in a diverse society.* Washington State University Administrative Intern Presentation.

Dressel, P. L., Johnson, F. D. & Marcus, P. M. (1970). *The confidence crisis.* San Francisco, CA: Jossey-Bass.

Drucker, P. F. (1974). *Management: Tasks, responsibilities, practice.* New York, NY: Harper & Row.

Dyer, W. G. (1977). *Team building: Issues and alternatives.* Reading, MA: Addison-Wesley.

Etzioni, A. (1964). *A comparative analysis of complex organizations: On power, involvement, and their correlates.* New York, NY: Free Press.

Fahey, L. & Christensen, H. K. (1989). Building distinctive competences into competitive advantages. In Liam Fahey (Ed.), *The strategic planning management reader.* Englewood Cliffs, NJ: Prentice-Hall.

Fisher, R. & Ury, W. (1983). *Getting to yes: Negotiating agreement without giving in.* New York, NY: Penguin Books.

French J. R. P., Jr. & Caplan. R. D. (1973). Organizational stress and individual strain. In A. J. Marrow (Ed.), *The failure of success.* New York, NY: AMACOM.

French, J. R. P. Jr. & Raven, B. (1968). The bases of social power. In D. Cartwright & A. Zander (Eds.), *Group dynamics: Research and theory.* New York, NY: Harper & Row.

Friedman, M. & Rosenman, R. (1974). *Type A behavior and your heart.* New York, NY: Alfred A. Knopf.

Gmelch, W. H. & Seedorf, R. (1989). Academic leadership under siege: The ambiguity and imbalance of department chairs. *Journal for Higher Education Management, 5(1),* 37-44.

Gmelch, W. H. & Burns, J. S. (April, 1991). *Sources of stress for academic department chairs: A national study.* Paper presented at the American Educational Research Association Conference, Chicago, IL. (ERIC:ED 339 306).

Gmelch, W. H. & Burns, J. S. (1993). The cost of academic leadership: Department chair stress. *Innovative Higher Education, 17(4),* 259-270.

Gmelch, W. H. & Wilke, P. K. (1991). The stresses of faculty and administrators in higher education. *Journal for Higher Education Management, 6(2),* 23-31.

Gmelch, W. H. (1982). *Beyond stress to effective management.* New York, NY: John Wiley and Sons.

Gmelch, W. H. (1991). Paying the price for academic leadership: Department chair tradeoffs. *Educational record,.* 72(3), 45-49.

Gmelch, W. H. & Carroll, J. B. (1991). The three R's of conflict management for department chairs and faculty. *Innovative Higher Education,* 16(2), 107-121.

Gmelch, W. H., Burns, J. S. , Carroll, J. B. , Harris, S. & Wentz, D. (1992). *Center for the study of the department chair: 1992 survey.* Pullman, WA: Washington State University.

Gmelch W. H., Carroll, J. B., Seedorf, R. & Wentz, D. (1990). *Center for the study of the department chair: 1990 survey.* Pullman, WA: Washington State University.

Gmelch, W. H., Lovrich, N. P. & Wilke, P. K. (1984). Stress in academe: A national perspective. *Research in Higher Education,* 20(4), 477-490.

Gmelch, W. H. & Miskin, V. D. (1984). *Productivity teams.* New York, NY: John Wiley & Sons, Inc.

Greiff, B. S. & Munther, P. K. (1980). *Tradeoffs: Executive, family and organizational life.* New York, NY: New American Library.

Hall, J. & Williams, M. S. (1966). A comparison of decision-making performances in established and ad hoc groups. *Journal of Personality and Social Psychology,* February, 214-222.

Hamel, G. & Prahalad, C. K. (1991). Strategic intent. In Joseph L. Bower (Ed.), *The craft of general management.* Boston, MA: Harvard Business School Publications, 144-164.

Hax, A. C. & Majluf, N. S. (1991). *The strategy concept and process: A pragmatic approach.* Englewood Cliffs, NJ: Prentice-Hall.

Hengstler, D. D., Brandenburg, D. C., Braskamp, L. A. & Smock, H. R. (1981). Faculty ratings as a measure of departmental and administrator quality. *Research in Higher Education.,* 14(3), 259-275.

Henry H. W. (1980). Appraising a company's strengths and weaknesses. *Managerial Planning,* July-August.

House, R. J. & Baetz, M. L. (1979). Some empirical generalizations and new research directions. In B.M. Staw (Ed.), *Research in organizational behavior,* Vol. 1., Greenwich, CT: JAI Press, 341-423.

Kahn, R., Wolfe, D. Quinn, R. & Snoek, R. (1964). *Organizational stress: Studies in role conflict and ambiguity.* New York, NY: John Wiley & Sons.

Kahn R. L., Wolfe, D. M., Quinn, R. P., Snoek, J. D. & Rosenthal, R. A. (1964). *Organizational stress: Studies in role conflict and ambiguity.* New York, NY: John Wiley & Sons.

Kanter, R. M. (1977). *Men and women of the corporation.* New York, NY: Basic Books.

Kanter R. M. (1983). *The change masters.* New York, NY: Simon & Schuster.

Katz, D. & Kahn, R. L. (1978). *Social psychology of organizations* (2nd ed.). New York, NY: John Wiley & Sons.

Katzell, R. A. & Guzzo, R. A. (1983). Psychology approaches to productivity improvement. *American Psychologist,* 38, 468-472.

Keller, G. (1983). *Academic strategy: The management revolution in higher education.* Baltimore, MD: The Johns Hopkins University Press.

Keys, B. & Case, T. (1990). How to become an influential manager. *Academy of Management Executive, 3,* 38-51.

Kouzes, J. M. & Posner, B. Z. (1987). *The leadership challenge: How to get extraordinary things done in organizations.* San Francisco, CA: Jossey-Bass.

Larson, C. E. & La Fasto, F. M. J. (1989). *Team work: What must go right/what can go wrong.* Newbury Park, CA: Sage Publications.

Latham, G. P. & Steele, T. P. (1983). The motivational effects of participation versus goal-setting on performance. *Academy of Management Journal, 18,* 824-845.

Latham, G. P. & Yukl, G. A. (1975). A review of research on the application of goal-setting in organizations. *Academy of Management Journal, 18,* 824-845.

Lawler, E. E., III. (1986). *High-involvement management: Participative strategies for improving organizational performance.* San Francisco, CA: Jossey-Bass..

Lee, D. E. (1985). Department chairpersons' perceptions of the role in three institutions. *Perception and Motor Skills, 61,* 23-49.

Lieberson, S. & O'Connor, J. F. (1972). Leadership and organizational performance: A study of large corporations. *American Sociological Review, 37,* 117-130.

Lincoln, W. & O'Donnell, R. (1986). *The course for mediators and impartial hearing officers.* Tacoma WA: National Center Associates.

Mackenzie, A. *(1990). The time trap.* New York, NY:AMACOM.

Markin, R. J. (1992). *CBE Dividend,* Washington State University, 9(1).

McLaughlin, G. W., Montgomery, J. R. & Malpass, L. F. (1975). Selected characteristics, roles, goals and satisfactions of department chairmen in state and land-grant institutions. *Research in Higher Education, 3,* 243-259.

Meredith, G. M. & Wunsch, M. A. (1991). The leadership of department chairpersons: Time resource management, rewards, frustrations, and role satisfaction. *Psychological Reports, 68, 451-454.*

Milstein, M. (1987). *Dilemmas in the chairpersons' role and what can be done about them.* Pullman, WA: Center for the Study of the Department Chair, Washington State University.

Miskin, V. D. & Gmelch, W. H. (1985). Quality leadership for quality teams. *Training and Development Journal,* 39(5), 122-130.

Moses, I. & Roe E. (1990). *Heads and chairs: Managing academic departments.*Queensland, Australia: University of Queensland Press.

Muczyk, J. P. & Reiman, B. C. (1987). The case for directive leadership. *The Academy of Management Executive,* 1(3), 301-311.

Naisbitt, J. & Aburdene, P. (1990). *Megatrends 2000.* New York, NY: William Morrow.

Nanus, B. (1992). *Visionary leadership.* San Francisco, CA: Jossey-Bass.

Oncken, W., Jr. & Wass, D. L. (1974). Management time: Who's got the monkey? *Harvard Business Review,* 52(6), 75-80.

Parker, G. M. (1991). *Team players and teamwork.* San Francisco, CA: Jossey-Bass.

Pearce, J. A., II & Robinson, R. B., Jr. (1989). *Management.* New York, NY: Random House.

Porter, M. E. (1991). How competitive forces shape strategy. In Joseph L. Bower (Ed.), *The craft of general management.* Boston, MA: Harvard Business School Publications, 77-88.

Raiffa, H. (1982). *The art and science of negotiation.* Cambridge, MA: The Belknap Press of Harvard University Press.

Randolph, A. & Posner, B. Z. (1988). *Effective project planning and management: Getting the job done.* Englewood Cliffs, NJ: Prentice-Hall.

Robbins, S. P. (1974). *Managing organizational conflict.* Englewood Cliffs, NJ: Prentice-Hall.

Seedorf, R. (1990). *Transition to leadership: The university department chair.* Unpublished doctoral dissertation, Washington State University.

Seyle, H. (1974). *Stress without distress.* Philadelphia, PA: J.G. Lippincott Co.

Simmel, G. (1955). *Conflict.* New York, NY: Free Press.

Smart, J. & Elton, J. (1976). Duties performed by department chairmen in Holland's model environments. *Journal of Educational Psychology,* 68(2), 194-204.

Smith, J. E., Carson K. P. & Alexander, R. A. (1984). Leadership: It can make a difference. *Academy of Management Journal , 27, 765-776.*

Steiner, G. A. (1979). *Strategic planning: What every manager should know.* New York, NY: Free Press.

Stoner, C. R. & Fry, F. L. (1987). *Strategic planning in the small business.* Cincinnati, OH: South-Western Publishing Co.

Sullivan, J. B. (1988). *Team origins.* Denver, CO: Performance Training Corp.

Thomas, K. W. (1976). Conflict and conflict management. In M. D. Dunnette (Ed.), *Handbook of industrial and organizational psychology.* Chicago, IL: Rand McNally.

Thomas, K. W. & Kilmann, R.L. (1974). *Thomas-Kilmann conflict mode instrument.* Xicom Incorporated.

Thompson, A. A., Jr. & Strickland, A. J., III. (1992). *Strategic management: Concepts and cases* (6th ed.). Homewood, IL: Richard D. Irwin.

Tucker, A. (1984). *Chairing the academic department: Leadership among peers* (2nd ed.). New York NY: American Council on Education/Macmillan.

Tucker, A. (1992). *Chairing the academic department: Leadership among peers* (3rd ed.). Phoenix, AZ: American Council on Education/Oryx.

Vroom, V. H. & Jago, A.. G. (1988). *The new leadership.* Englewood Cliffs, NJ: Prentice-Hall.

Walton, R. E. & Dutton, J. M. (1969). The management of interpersonal conflict: A model and review. *Administrative Science Quarterly,* (March), 73-84.

Weiner, N. & Mahoney, T. A. (1981). A model of corporate performance as a function of environmental, organizational, and leadership influences. *Academy of Management Journal,* 24, 453-470.

Wilke, P. K., Gmelch, W. H. & Lovrich, N. P. (1985). Stress and productivity: Evidence of the inverted U-function. *Public Productivity Review,* 9(4), 342-356.

Williams, M. J., Jr. (1985). The management of conflict. In R. J. Fecher (Ed.), *Applying corporate management strategies: New dimensions for higher education,* No. 50. San Francisco, CA: Jossey-Bass.

Yavitz, B. & Newman, W. H. (1982). *Strategy in action.* New York, NY: Free Press.

Yukl, G. A. (1981). *Leadership in organizations.* Englewood Cliffs, NJ: Prentice-Hall.

Index